CW01023351

AUTISM FROM A TO Z

An #actuallyautistic book
for families and professionals
that curates the latest information
on autism spectrum neurologies

KATHY CARTER

PRESENTED BY

SPECTRA BLOG

Autism from A to Z

An #actuallyautistic book
for families and professionals
that curates the latest information
on autism spectrum neurologies

By Kathy Carter

Presented by SPECTRA.BLOG

ISBN: 978-0-9934392-5-4
Also available for Kindle

Copyright 2020 Kathy Carter

The rights of Kathy Carter to be identified as the author of this work, have been asserted in accordance with the Copyright, Designs and Patents Act 1998. All rights reserved. No part of this publication may be reproduced, stored in or introduced into a retrieval system, or transmitted in any form, or by any means (electronic, mechanical, photocopying, recording or otherwise), without prior permission of the author. Any person who does any unauthorized act in relation to this publication may be liable to criminal prosecution and civil claims for damages. First Published in 2019 by Sirenia Books (www.sireniabooks.com). A division of Sirenia Ltd.

Cover design and page layout by Lighthouse24

Contents

Preface

I wrote this *#actuallyautustic* book as a collation of articles from my *www.spectra.blog* website, to help enlighten interested parties. I had been dismayed at the widespread lack of awareness, acceptance and education concerning autism, which in my experience, incorporates professionals including doctors, counsellors and educators, as well as the general public. This lack of awareness, acceptance and education is presumably simply down to a lack of exposure to modern concepts concerning autism.

This book is written in layperson's language, and each chapter, which covers a key facet of autism, includes a section titled 'The autist's view', for a first-hand viewpoint. The content aims to be modern and forward-thinking, acknowledging the neurodiversity standpoint, and moving on from old views and stereotypes about autists. On that note, I use the word 'autist' as a shorthand to describe an autistic individual. This isn't necessarily a widely used term – others use the approbative nouns 'autistic', 'aspie' (e.g. shorthand for someone diagnosed with Asperger Syndrome), or autie, for example. 'Autist' is just my personal preference!

Although I delve in more detail in the chapter: *'L is for labels and language'* regarding the subject of what language to use when discussing autistic people, the viewpoints within this book are my own; and respectfully, I would propose that I am entitled to these opinions, even though others may have differing opinions, and may self-identify (as an autist) in a different way to myself.

Throughout the book, I have included weblinks to relevant sources of information (which are also available as live links at the website: *www.spectra.blog/resources)*.

Despite being an autist living in a neurodivergent household, and having undertaken educational studies into autism, I don't consider myself to be an expert. For expert knowledge, I would point readers to authors such as Dr. Ross Greene, and his book: 'The Explosive Child' (by HarperCollins – *www.tiny.cc/Ross_Greene*); and author Steve Silberman, whose book, 'Neurotribes' proffers fascinating autism back-history (by Allen & Unwin – *www.tiny.cc/Neurotribes*). There are also many autistic advocates writing online about the way they see the world, using hashtags like #actuallyautistic and #askanautistic; their experiences are invaluable.

I would also like to add the following disclaimer: The information, including but not limited to text, graphics, images, videos and other material contained on the: *www.spectra.blog* website, the accompanying Facebook page: *www.facebook.com/autismblogging*, and within this book: '*Autism from A-Z*', are for informational purposes only. The purpose of the author's aforementioned platforms and this book is to share information from an autistic perspective. Individuals reading this book, as well as my articles and information, should always seek the care of a qualified doctor or relevant healthcare professional to discuss their own personal healthcare status or that of their families.

I hope you enjoy the book; I suggest first reading the chapter: '*A is for autism*', before reading the other chapters at will; they are alphabetical, and do not need to be read in order. At the end of the book is a poem I wrote called 'A thousand souls', which I hope is a fitting close to the title, that people will enjoy.

Finally, my grateful thanks go to my professional reviewers, including Chloe, Emily May, Lorraine, Sofia and Tazmin.

A is for autism

This book is a layperson's guide to autism, from an autist's perspective. Why write a book on autism? Because many resources are written by people who may be academic experts, but don't have that first-person viewpoint; furthermore, understanding of autism from a neurodiversity perspective has advanced dramatically in the last few years, meaning that some older material is limited in its viewpoint. This book aims to provide families, educators, autists and any interested parties with a balanced, modern view of autism. (See the chapter: '*N is for neurodiversity*').

Each alphabetical chapter within this book represents a key feature of autism, and is sourced from the popular *www.spectra.blog* website. This first chapter is a brief introduction to the main facets of autism – what it is (and is not); the diagnostic criteria; autism labels and language; and the key areas that form the basis of what it means to be diagnosed as autistic. Autism is of course explored in more detail in each chapter of the book; and at the end of each chapter, the author shares perspective and autistic experiences.

Before diving in, it is worth mentioning that there are currently many differences of opinion concerning what is seen as the medicalisation and pathologising of autism. Most autism researchers and experts referenced by health bodies and medical influencers used this paradigm. Historically and diagnostically, autism has been regarded as a set of deficits. It is not within this author's remit to examine the historical theories of autism, however a book reproduced online, that looks at the social history of autism, provides many links and references – (source: *www.tiny.cc/BEvans*). It is fair to say that many autistic individuals now prefer that, instead of solely deficits, the characteristics of autism, both positive and negative, are considered.

Of course, this author advocates this paradigm, but equally understands that those individuals learning about autism, particularly parents and healthcare professionals, need to start with a knowledge-base about diagnostic criteria and the main features of autism as recognised by healthcare clinicians. From there, with this rudimentary knowledge, we are all able to research and gain understanding regarding the more modern theories and paradigms.

Let's start at the beginning, with the question – what is autism? To describe it in its most basic form, autism is now widely thought to be a lifelong difference in neurological processing.

* The UK's National Autistic Society (NAS) states that autism is: '*A lifelong, developmental condition that affects how a person communicates with and relates to other people, and how they experience the world around them.*'

* The UK's National Health Service (NHS) states: '*Being autistic does not mean you have an illness or disease. It means your brain works in a different way from other people.*'

* Autism does not equate to low intellect. Statistics vary according to source, but around half of all autistic individuals are said to have average to above average intellectual ability. The NAS puts the number of autistic individuals with co-existing, intellectual disabilities – defined by the NHS as: '*Disorders*

characterised by reduced ability to understand complex information [and] significant impairment of adaptive / social functioning, affecting development' (source: *www.tiny.cc/Definition_Disabilities*) – at between 44-52%.

The charity Mencap also quotes around 50% – source: *www.tiny.cc/mencap_autism*). However, a recent American study (source: *www.tiny.cc/GNSoke*) looked at the prevalence of co-occurring conditions in autistic children, finding that cognitive developmental disability – a term that encompasses intellectual disability, and also disabilities that can affect cognitive and physical functioning – was present in just 15.6% of the autistic children in the study. So to reiterate – autism does not equate to low intellect.

* Speech and communication differences are not necessarily indicators of intellectual ability. *'Communication is a complex cognitive and motor activity. The act of communicating can be verbal or non-verbal, or a combination of both. These skills are developmental and have a number of components. Communication includes semantics (understanding the meaning of words) and pragmatics (social use) of language'*, explains a study titled 'Language disorders and Autism' (source: *www.tiny.cc/WRAY*). The modern way of looking at autism, which is gaining increasing, widespread support as a valid school of thought, sees cognitive developmental disabilities and genetic disorders that an autistic individual has classed as co-existing conditions (see the chapter: *'C is for co-existing conditions'*). Co-existing conditions associated with autism can affect communication in various ways – some autists may be non-verbal, with apraxia of speech.

This is when speech movement (coordinated via the brain, to the lips, jaw and tongue) itself is difficult or impossible. (Although research continues on the subject of whether apraxia is a co-existing condition, or a result of autists' 'social reciprocity challenges', e.g. somehow part of the autism itself, stemming from a difference in the structure of that individual's temporal lobe, the area of the brain involved in auditory perception – source: *www.tiny.cc/SpeechApraxia*). But to be clear: a speech or communication difference is not an indicator of intellectual ability.

* Anxiety disorders (see the chapter: *'A is for anxiety'*), are common in autists; however this fact doesn't make autism a mental illness in itself.

So, we have looked at what autism is not. Today, autism is widely considered to be a set of neurology configurations affecting the individual's processing abilities (we will look into the features of autism further into the book), at varying levels – hence the term 'spectrum' – so, no two autists are the same!

One interesting theory (developed by Kamila and Henry Markram, and Tania Rinaldi) proposes that autism is not a mental deficit, but a mental overload, and that autistic children especially deal with the mental overload by trying to shut off the outside world. The Intense World Theory proposes that autism may be described by hyper-perception, hyper-attention and hyper-memory, with the brain's major functions working at increased capacity that leaves little 'energy' for social interactions. The Intense World Theory also supports the idea that rather than a lack of empathy, as proposed by so-called (usually neurotypical or NT/non-autistic) experts for decades, autists experience over-sensitivity in the field of empathetic responses. Followers of the Intense World Theory suggest that autistic children would better suit calm environments that do not add to this mental overload, and that autists have greatly enhanced perception, attention and memory. (Sources: *www.tiny.cc/IntenseWorld* and *www.tiny.cc/IntenseWorld2*). Many autists agree with the concepts behind these theories, and the idea of hyperfunctioning of neural circuitry, and a state of over-arousal for autistic individuals. However, the theory has drawn its detractors, notably as some studies were based on animals, not humans; and large-scale studies developing these early theories (dating from 2007) are (unfortunately) seemingly lacking.

As autism is not a medical illness, there are no treatments or cures (source: *http://nhs.uk*).

Autistic individuals generally experience differences in two key processing areas: (1) differences in social communication / interaction; and (2) restricted or repetitive thought patterns, imaginative behaviours, interests or activities. (Now often thought of as monotropism, or 'atypical patterns of attention' – source: *www.tiny.cc/DMurray*). Clinicians now also increasingly recognise a third area of processing difference; brain responses to sensory stimulation. (We will come onto these key areas further in this chapter).

Incidentally, autism was previously defined by a 'triad of impairments', a concept introduced in the late 1970s by Wing and Gould – see also the chapter '*W is for Lorna Wing*'. The concept focussed on three areas of difference: communication and language; social and emotional interaction, and flexible imaginative functions (including repetitive behaviours). The triad and the theories that followed also described challenges in so-called 'theory of mind' (attributing mental states to others); executive function (regulating organisational cognitive processes); and a propensity to detail-focused behaviour. However, this triad concept has since been referred to as a 'transitional' idea, in the context of psychiatric history (source: *www.tiny.cc/cashin-triad*).

Let's now look at the diagnostic criteria for autism, and some of the issues concerning labels and language, before re-visiting the differences in the areas of social communication / interaction, atypical attention patterns and sensory challenges.

Both the current draft of the ICD-11 (ICD being short for the World Health Organisation's 'International Statistical Classification of Diseases and Health Related Problems' (source: *www.tiny.cc/_ICD11*), and the DSM-5 (DSM being short for the American Psychiatric Association's 'Diagnostic and Statistical Manual of Mental Disorders' (source: *www.tiny.cc/DSM-5*), advise diagnosing clinicians to use the broad term Autism Spectrum Disorder (ASD), for diagnosis. However, outside of diagnostic circles and in everyday parlance, 'autism' or 'autism spectrum neurology' are generally preferred terms.

Although the two manuals vary, essentially, diagnosing clinicians are advised to choose relevant sub-categories for the autistic individual that relate to any co-existing conditions of intellect or language. The DSM-5 uses numbered categories detailing the levels of support required, while the ICD-11 uses sub-categories. (The current ICD-11, at the time of writing, is still apparently inviting clinicians' proposals and comments).

Let's briefly now move onto autism labels and language. Unfortunately, some training providers, resource materials, clinicians and families (at the time of writing) are still referring to out of date functioning terms such as: 'mild', 'severe', 'low functioning' and 'high functioning' within the context of autism profiles. It is this author's view that 'severe' and 'mild' are not very helpful terms. They suggest a linear line of autism that gets progressively more mild or severe, which is a dated concept.

Autism is more widely being seen now as a set of internal processing differences. If the autistic individual has additional co-existing conditions that debilitate their life, advocates of the neurodiversity model maintain that it is these conditions that affect the individual's support needs.

'Has high support needs' and 'has low support needs' are therefore better phrases to use than 'severe' or 'mild', as they refer to the person's needs, rather than trying to 'rate' or scale their autism. 'Severe autism' was commonly used (generally not by the autist themselves!) to describe an autistic individual who also had co-existing conditions that may include cognitive, intellectual and / or speech difficulties. Meanwhile, 'mild autism' described a supposed high-functioning autist, e.g. someone who was perceived as socially fitting in well within (and functioning and communicating well within) their environment. However, these definitions created clear differences of opinion and confusion, and only described others' perception of the autist's 'functionality', not the individual's actual capacity. (See the chapter 'L is for labels and language').

(Interestingly, Robert Chapman, writing on Psychology for Today (source: *www.tiny.cc/RChapman*), recently proposed 'making better make sense of autistic disablement' by drawing on the notion of intersectionality, developed by feminist theorist, Kimberlé Crenshaw. Mr. Chapman suggests using phrasing drawn from intersectional feminism, and applying it within the framing of cognitive disability; e.g., to quote Mr. Chapman: *'When someone is, say, autistic and learning disabled, then they [could be considered to be] part of a third intersectional category (i.e. that of 'learning disabled autistics')… This framing allows us to acknowledge the complexity of autism without dehumanising different disabilities under the term 'severe', and [avoids] autistic people 'talking over' those autistic people with intersecting disabilities. For on this model, the only people who should be taken as the voice of any given intersectional identity are those that fall within their intersection.')*

One issue to consider is that in cases where 'severe' is used to describe an individual's autism, it is often unlikely that the individual themselves has a say in how they're being described. The vast majority of autists are able to communicate somehow, and if it is not through verbalisation, then there are various communication devices, as well as writing and typing, that would allow the autist some input into the language that's used to describe them. A further issue is that calling someone's autism mild, or saying that they are high functioning, undermines their challenges. All that is being described by the term 'high functioning' is how other individuals perceive the autist; e.g. how 'typically' the autist functions, when compared to NT individuals. Just because the autist has learned how to appear 'functional' in a given environment (see the chapter: *'M is for masking'*), doesn't mean their internal neurological challenges are mild. (Having said that, there may be times when it is useful to use functional labelling in context, to aid others' understanding and educate them, and to help with access to support and services for an individual autist). Readers may like to read the chapters *'U is for understanding the autism filter'* and *'V is for visualising autism'*, which try to elaborate on how an autistic person sees and experiences the world.

Let's now revisit the three main features of autism:

Issues with expected social communication and social interaction

As a child, difficulties with social communication and social interaction can be crushing. This is why an early autism diagnosis can help, e.g. to get supports in place at the child's place of education. (The communicative area of autistic processing difficulty is likely to affect the individual's anxiety levels too, as many autists are prone to anxious episodes). Autists may lack emotional calibration, and may not have the intrinsic understanding and prediction of others' social behaviours, meaning they mis-read social situations, and also language. However, many autists are at peace with the differences that their social communication and social interaction issues bring. They may for example very much enjoy their own company; and the fact that they're not compelled to take part in the social minutiae of daily integration is not necessarily a bad thing, if it leaves the autist more time to enjoy their interests, and interactions with close friends and family members. (See the chapter: 'C is for communication'.)

Restriction, repetition and atypical attention patterns

These elements, which include so-called 'flexible imaginative functions', are experienced in different ways; from hyper-focusing on a special interest (also described as monotropism, or 'atypical patterns of attention' – source: *www.tiny.cc/DMurray*) to adopting repetitive processes, including 'stims'. (See the chapters: 'S is for special interest', and 'S is for stimming' for more information).

The National Autistic Society states: '*Repetitive behaviour and routines can be a source of enjoyment... and a way of coping with everyday life. But they may also limit people's involvement in other activities, and cause distress or anxiety.*'

It is however worthwhile noting that the 'rigidity of thought' seen in autists can be beneficial, e.g. leading to pattern-spotting, problem-solving and organisation. Hyper-focus may lend itself to excellence in a field, for example in a sporting or artistic capacity, where practice is required. The author discusses black and white thinking styles in the chapter: '*B is for black and white thinking*').

Sensory challenges

A further key factor for autists is the presence of sensory issues, e.g. over or under-sensitivity to sounds, touch, light, temperatures etc. Autistic people often have difficulty processing everyday sensory information, and any of the senses may be over or under-sensitive (or both) at different times. The 'ultra-sensitivity to sensory input' theory sees some environments negatively affecting autistic individuals, making them feel tired and sensitive. Excessive sensory overwhelm is therefore a big factor in autistic meltdown (see the chapter '*M is for meltdown*'), when an autist's system is overloaded by factors such as excessive expectations, extensive socialisation and routine changes, and sensory overload.

Sensory challenges were seemingly not given enough credence historically, in terms of how greatly an autist is affected by them. However, the great strides by autistic advocates, in terms of creating books, blogs and vlogs describing their experiences, has illustrated the importance of managing one's sensory challenges, as an autist. (See the chapter: '*S is for sensory*'). While sensory differences can present difficulties, with all of life's noise, colour and 'busyness', there are positives to be taken from the unique sensory experiences that some autists experience. For example, some autists experience amazing phenomena that stem from their sensory differences, from their definitions of colours and sounds, to the way they hear and process music.

The autist's view

Regarding the elements covered in this chapter, it is important for the layperson to understand that autism is, at its core, widely thought to be a difference in processing. It is a filter through which autists experience the world. Additional issues such as cognitive developmental difficulties and mental health challenges can be present alongside autism (e.g. as a co-existing condition); but modern theories propose that they are not in themselves autism. It is also important for people to understand that functioning labels are generally not helpful; it's dismissive to say my autism 'must be mild', because I can function well societally.

Concerning the main autistic features, expected social communication and social interactions leave me most challenged. Large groups of people, places where 'chit-chat' is expected, or anyone that I am expected to talk to, but don't know what to talk about, can be anxiety-inducing. But my outlook, perhaps considered anti-social on occasion, does leave me more time or 'head-space' to enjoy my interests, and to be selective about who I chat to, and most importantly, when. It is interesting to consider the issue of 'emotional reciprocity' when discussing social communication and interactions. In the chapter *'C is for communication'*, I look at the issue of how autists converse with others. According to expert lecturers like Dr. Damian Milton and Dr. Luke Beardon, there's a concept called 'double empathy'. It helps clarify why, when people with different experiences of the world interact, they may struggle to connect. Studies by University of Edinburgh researcher Dr. Catherine Crompton and her colleagues (source: *www.tiny.cc/Crompton*) show that NT people may be less willing to interact socially with autistic people. Equally, autists are more willing to interact socially with fellow autistic individuals. As detailed later in this book, it seems we're all more comfortable when conversing with our own neurotype! This theory does make sense to me, and many of my friends, even though they're NT, are what I would call 'attuned to the more sensitive mind'. As many autists feel 'out of place', it is good to know that difficulties with emotional reciprocity can actually be down to both parties conversing.

Restricted or repetitive thought patterns can be limiting; we autists thrive on routine, and the tiniest change can throw our whole day out from an emotional perspective. However, there's often an element of control and comfort in the regularity of repetitive behaviours and the act of 'scheduling'. (If one engages in unhelpful thought patterns, in my experience there are ways to help break the pattern, e.g. brain-training concepts like the Lightning Process – see: *www.lightningprocess.com* – which utilises one's brain to improve body health.)

From a sensory point of view, any of the senses may be over or under-sensitive at different times, for autists. In my case, this leaves me feeling pretty capable on some days, but more challenged on others. On hyper-sensitive days, I find noise especially difficult. Every little sound can be grating and annoying, making me wince and cringe. There's a real risk of sensory overload. Some things – the sound of someone eating, a clock ticking – can be incredibly annoying and will affect my mood. On under-sensitive days, I specifically like to listen to loud rock music; it helps my brain to recalibrate. (Some children may 'sensory seek' on those days, with physical, hyper-behaviour to stimulate their senses).

I was interested to read more about the Intense World Theory; many individuals like myself agree that concepts of hyper-functioning, over-arousal and excessive empathy fit very well with the autistic experience. I look forward to more studies being conducted in this field.

A is for Asperger Syndrome

Asperger's is the autistic profile that describes autists with Asperger Syndrome, a term coined by Psychiatrist Lorna Wing in the 1980s (see the chapter: *'W is for Wing (Lorna Wing)'*. It is named after the Austrian paediatrician Hans Asperger. Wing was a pioneer in the field of childhood developmental conditions, and published a ground-breaking paper in the journal Psychological Medicine on Hans Asperger in 1981, which introduced the term 'Asperger Syndrome' to the English-speaking world for the first time. However, while many autists have an Asperger's diagnosis (and some still self-identify as 'aspie'), clinicians generally don't issue new autism diagnoses with this profile, to meet the latest guidelines. Dr. Asperger first characterised autistic children with distinct psychological differences (but typical or high levels of intelligence) in 1938, and published his autism papers in 1944. However, Hans Asperger's name is now consciously being removed from the medical lexicon, following recent evidence collated by a medical historian that revealed Dr. Asperger was an active Nazi collaborator, and cooperated with their child euthanasia programme. (For more information on the early years of autism's history, including Dr. Asperger's contributions, this author strongly recommends reading American writer and autism expert Steve Silberman's book, 'Neurotribes'; a very well-written piece of autism back-history! Visit: *www.tiny.cc/Neurotribes)*.

The autist's view

Many autists like myself identify as having Asperger Syndrome, and do often still feel comfortable with the Asperger's diagnostic 'label', despite the revelations about Dr. Asperger. The term 'aspie' is still widely used and liked by some autists, and I believe it has a self-deprecating element that allows further discussion with friends and family members about autism. No-one condones Dr. Asperger's history, however the issue of connotations because an individual syndrome or condition is named after a particular person are complex. Personally, if the term 'Wing Syndrome' (after Lorna Wing) was proposed, I wouldn't have an issue with this, as her contribution to autism research is incomparable. However on the whole, the decision to use a single diagnostic umbrella for autism, (e.g. encompassing autistic profiles that would previously have been described as 'Asperger Syndrome') is helpful, if it aids education that autism is essentially the autist's core, or their metaphorical internal computer processor. (NB, other issues, e.g. co-existing conditions and cognitive developmental disabilities, can perhaps be considered as additional computer programmes or apps, if we're continuing the computing analogy!) I discuss these concepts further in the chapter: *L is for labels and language*.

To conclude, I feel that separating the autistic profiles, e.g. with some individuals designated diagnostically as having Asperger's, was ultimately not helpful; although I am personally comfortable with the Asperger's diagnostic 'label'.

A is for anxiety

Anxiety and other mental health problems are rife in the 21st-century, but for many people the issues are episodic, or caused by obvious external factors.

The charity Anxiety UK reports that anxiety disorders are very common, with one in six adults regularly experiencing some form of 'neurotic health problem', and the most common neurotic disorders being anxiety and depressive disorders. More than one in 10 people in the general population are likely to have a 'disabling anxiety disorder' at some stage in their life, reports the organisation. (Source: *www.anxietyuk.org.uk*).

However, if you are autistic, for many individuals, anxiety can really be considered to be part of your autistic DNA. Definitive statistics and figures that indicate anxiety levels among autists vary; there's also the issue that many individuals' anxiety isn't necessarily logged with their doctor; they may just live with it. The National Autistic Society (NAS) advises that anxiety is very common in autists, citing that around 79% of autistic adults experience mental health issues, while two in five autistic people are diagnosed with an anxiety disorder; they state that around 42% of autistic children (compared with just 3% of children without autism) experience anxiety. They also agree that autistic children and young people can experience a high 'base level' of anxiety every day, while some studies put the figure of how many autistic people experience anxiety at up to 84% (source: *www.tiny.cc/v_Postorino*).

The information resource Spectrum News described that the reason we see 'classic things' like social phobia and generalised anxiety in autists is because people on the autistic spectrum have unique, distinct ways of perceiving the world. They reported in 2017 that Psychologist Connor Kerns, assistant professor at the A.J. Drexel Autism Institute in Philadelphia, USA, is working with others on new ways to measure both ordinary and unusual forms of anxiety in autistic people. (There are links to Kerns' and others' studies on anxiety and autism at: *www.tiny.cc/kerns*).

So, is a degree of anxiety an inbuilt factor for someone who is autistic? Through this author's communication with other autistic individuals, and from collating information, it seems that a substantial degree of anxiety is an inbuilt factor with autism – a given, if you will. Many autists would for example describe their anxiety (on a scale of 1-10) at being at five, just as a baseline. Just getting through the day with all of the run-of-the-mill, usual challenges can be very stressful for autists; it is as if our neutral state is to have a certain level of anxiety.

If you know about autism, then the reasons for anxiety are obvious. Probably a major factor is social masking – trying to fit in with the world, and say and do things that others consider appropriate – which can be exhausting and stressful. If you are an undiagnosed autist, there is the constant feeling of being different and not fitting in, or failing at being your best self. Very stressful! If you are a child, this is compounded by all of the developmental issues, and social and educational expectations. Just the neurological differences for autists, in terms of elements like executive function, memory, sensory issues, emotional calibration and communication, can bring about a sense of anxiety. And all this is without all of the usual stresses concerning finances, places of education, workplaces, relationships and so on, that life brings.

For a child who is educated at school, the pressures of fitting in and completing school work when you have issues like executive function difficulties and possibly other co-existing conditions can be immensely stressful and anxiety-inducing.

One *www.spectra.blog* follower, #adhdgirl from #theadhdlife, has a diagnosis of autism as well as Attention Deficit Hyperactivity Disorder (ADHD) and dyspraxia, the latter being a difficulty in activities requiring coordination and movement. *"I have had constant anxiety about one thing or another, for my entire life – there are very few moments of my life where I'm not totally absorbed one way or another by some extreme worry,"* she explains. *"This can even be because things are not in their right place, or I have a too-long list of chores, or I have a short appointment to attend one day that week. It would be nice to have a break from that constant pressure and anxiety, but for me, it gets worse the older I get,"* she concludes. It is no wonder that unexplained anxiety is often one of the first things that parents of undiagnosed autistic children notice. And it is no surprise that so many children hold it together emotionally at school, and let out their frustrations at home, leading to unhelpful third party comments like: *'Well, he / she doesn't seem to be very anxious at school.'*

One aspect of managing anxiety as an autist (of any age) is knowing your own autistic spectrum. But what does this author mean by this? It means: what triggers you; what overloads you in a sensory or social capacity; what external factors cause frustration; anger or upset; what sensory challenges affect your mood? What activities that you are engaged in (whether this is social activities, or within the educational action setting, workplace etc) make you stressed? Which family members, friends, associates or workplace colleagues are drains or fountains? (Drains being the people who drain you of your emotional energy, and fountains being the people who replenish it). Would it be feasible to stay away from the drains to a degree, no matter who they are? Or is there a way to educate the people around you further about what you need to do to reduce your anxiety day-to-day, in a self-care capacity?

There are of course age-appropriate medications available for anxiety, in addition to therapies, dietary and exercise interventions and natural remedies. (As stated in this book's preface, individuals should always seek the care of a qualified doctor or relevant healthcare professional to discuss their own personal healthcare status, or that of their families.)

But let's look at the issue of triggers for anxiety simply – if you had a severe allergic reaction to a type of animal or a plant, would you constantly be in close proximity to the animal or plant? Would you take a job in that field? It would be inadvisable, for your health. Yet many of us who are autistic continue to do things that cause an unpleasant reaction to our bodies. Many of us keep doing things that induce anxiety. As do many parents of autistic children. Anxiety is a psychological response which can have physiological consequences; noticing one's triggers, or the triggers for a child, is a massive step on the road to managing anxiety.

Anxiety that builds up is a big factor for an autist heading to meltdown, shutdown or even autistic burnout. (See the relevant chapters: 'M is for meltdown', 'S is for shutdown', and 'B is for burnout'). Stories abound of young autistic adults reaching key developmental stages in their life, for example the start of high school or the start of university, and then having some sort of emotional breakdown. Noticing one's own anxiety levels can be immensely helpful in preventing these incredibly detrimental occurrences. For example, noticing: changes in appetite or interest in food; an increase in harmful repetitive processes (including thoughts), as well as self-stimulating behaviours that are detrimental; general apathy and lethargy; a lack of patience with people and reduced ability to socialise to one's usual capacity; and even a change in one's heartbeat, if you use a health / activity tracker.

In children, are they 'acting out' a little more (behaviour that challenges is often a big 'red flag' sign); or having more meltdowns, or episodes of sadness? These can be signs of raised anxiety levels. Are they finding it harder to regulate their emotions; withdrawing into themselves; exhibiting more self-soothing 'stims'; having difficulties in their place of education; becoming more controlling of their environment, or experiencing increased levels of perfectionism? Helping autistic children to identify their own responses can be very useful. If a child is experiencing any significant number of the above signs, it could be time to reduce their sensory challenges and levels of socialisation, reduce the demands put upon them, and do whatever is needed to help them recalibrate in a safe place, with plenty of downtime that meets their needs.

The autist's view

Personally speaking, I can say that my anxiety never really goes away, but it is manageable. However, this has only really come about with an autism diagnosis. Talking therapies, practices like pilates and yoga, as well as mindfulness (please however see my comments on mindfulness, on page 148), can help, but really a major factor is to know your own autistic spectrum. That is, when you're over or under stimulated from a sensory perspective; how much downtime is scheduled after a heavy dose of socialisation; and whether the workload (whether it's concerning the workplace, education, or day to day chores) is too much. Anxiety and low mood is essentially the body's way of showing you that you are asking too much of it, in my experience. I have found some over-the-counter, natural remedies to be useful, and take one that includes fish oil, sunflower oil and lecithin. I give my son age-appropriate multivitamins, as they may be recommended for children; vitamin C in particular is known to play an important therapeutic role for anxiety – (source: *www.tiny.cc/Oliveira*). As mentioned, individuals should always seek the care of a qualified doctor or relevant healthcare professional to discuss their own personal healthcare status, or that of their families.

Some probiotic supplements are said to help maintain health; the NHS cautiously says: 'There's some evidence that probiotics may be helpful in some cases'. There's also an increasing amount of information available on a proposed gut-brain connection (source: *www.tiny.cc/harvard-health*). However, any sources proposing that autism and so-called 'symptoms' are the result of gut issues are (to date), unsubstantiated. Such links have even led to disturbing practices that harm autists. Both the National Institute for Health and Care Excellence (NICE) and the NHS therefore advise parents and carers not to subject autistic individuals to any kind of exclusion diets, in order to 'manage autistic symptoms'. (See also pg 48).

As an (undiagnosed autistic) child, I experienced several anxiety-related issues, including episodes of hyperventilation and a recurring metabolic condition that was probably linked to the excessive release of stress hormones. Thankfully nowadays families and clinicians are much better equipped to look at the reasons behind physical symptoms that may originate from anxiety. The body is after all a holistic entity, and looking after both mind and body can only be a good thing.

If the statistics stating that 42% of autistic children (compared with just 3% of children without autism) experience anxiety are true (and I dare say the figures could be even higher), we owe it to our autistic children to take their mental health seriously. I believe that unexplained anxiety can be a useful red flag for neurodevelopmental conditions in children, and managing an autistic child's triggers (just as I explained in the above section, e.g. concerning sensory and socialisation challenges), and making a note of factors like diet, sleep and environmental factors, can be useful.

I also believe it is imperative that neurodivergent children educated at school have educators familiar with their neurology and its implications, to observe if the child's anxiety levels increase. (The signs can be subtle, e.g. tics such as heavy blinking, emotional or social withdrawal, unexplained physiological symptoms like a tummy ache, or a reluctance to undertake a supposed 'fun' or highly-anticipated activity). School refusal itself would be a big red flag that the child's emotional and cognitive skillsets are overshadowed and exceeded by the various demands experienced at school, at the time in question.

(Families reporting that a child's anxiety 'spikes' at home, when the child is reportedly non-anxious at school, should also be taken seriously, as the issue of 'masking' at school and 'letting it out' in the safety and 'sameness' of their home is commonplace, for many neurodivergent children).

A is for autism and ADHD

In the chapter '*C is for co-existing conditions*', we briefly touch on Attention Deficit Hyperactivity Disorder (ADHD). However, the condition is also worth exploring in more detail here, because a dual diagnosis of autism and ADHD (both neurodevelopmental differences) is becoming more prevalent now, due to clinicians' ability to diagnose both neurologies under the latest diagnostic criteria, and also due to an increase in clinicians' experience and exposure to individual people with both neurologies. (It is worth noting however that receiving a dual diagnosis at the same time is not yet prevalent – more commonly, the individual has two separate appointments).

The older (since updated) DSM-4 (the American Psychiatric Association's 'Diagnostic and Statistical Manual of Mental Disorders') reportedly specified that an autism diagnosis was an 'exclusion criterion' for ADHD, thereby limiting research in the field (source: *www.tiny.cc/YLeitner*). The reason why the two neurologies may co-occur is unknown, however there's thought to be some common underlying aetiology, as yet unconfirmed.

It does require a very experienced clinician or multi-disciplinary team to carry out the assessment and subsequent diagnosis of both autism and ADHD, as the two neurologies presenting together can make diagnosis much harder. But why is it harder to spot an individual with autism and ADHD – for example, if you're a teacher or family member? Here's a theory – is it as if the two extremes of each neurology can appear to be 'softened', or can become less noticeable to outsiders? (Inside, the challenges and conflicts the individual experiences can of course be considerable – but the outer 'presentation' can perhaps sometimes appear more typical). An example of this theory is that autists typically prefer sticking to their routines and are likely to only gradually increase their limitations; whereas those with ADHD may be more impulsive and fearless – could the two extremes potentially mean the individual's choice at a given time (e.g. to climb a high and unknown tree) sits more in the middle? Is it possible that an individual with a dual diagnosis may be less likely to avoid a new activity as it is out of their 'safe' and 'known' remit of 'sameness' (relating to autism); but also less likely to take a big or dangerous risk (relating to ADHD / impulsivity)? E.g. the two 'personalities' offset each other, somewhat?

A Consultant Community Paediatrician specialising in autism and ADHD told this author: *"Children with both autism and ADHD can often face more serious challenges than people with either diagnosis alone: They can have greater impairments in adaptive functioning, a term that refers to self-care and daily living skills, and more severe social and cognitive issues. It is also recognised that children and young people with both autism and ADHD are more at risk of developing anxiety and mood disturbance than children who have only autism or ADHD alone. However, some children with both conditions can sometimes appear to be less affected than they would be with a single diagnosis, as in many ways having both conditions can help to compensate for some of the challenges that the individual conditions raise. For example, verbal impulsivity from ADHD can help the child with their social communication, or can appear to help, leading to the risk of underestimating the child's difficulties. Some children with both diagnoses do not show the same level of repetitive and restricted interests as those with autism alone, because of their inattention – they may be too busy and active to be repetitive in their actions. Equally, the caution and need for control that some autistics have can moderate some of the impulsive acts associated with ADHD. Equally however, [the dual diagnosis] can be extremely problematic, as many autistic children who want life to be predictable and routine-based, and to be in control, will find that their ADHD makes this very difficult."*

It is said that some children with both neurologies are unfortunately having their autism missed, if they get an ADHD diagnosis first. In a study in the journal 'Paediatrics', researchers looked at around 1,500 autistic children (source: *www.tiny.cc/asd-adhd*). They found that those who got an ADHD diagnosis before an autism diagnosis were diagnosed as being autistic an average of three years later than those who got the autism diagnosis first. They were 30 times more likely to get the autism diagnosis when they were aged six or older.

Let's now look at the key factors of both autism and ADHD. ADHD is defined by impaired functioning in the areas of attention, hyperactivity, and impulsivity. Often, children with ADHD have difficulty focusing on one activity or task; they may be easily distracted; they are often physically unable to sit still. As with autism, children with ADHD often have difficulty moving their attention to other activities, when they are asked to do so.

As we explain elsewhere, autism is characterised by social and communicative difficulties, restrictive/repetitive processes and behaviours, and sensory challenges. Autistic children are likely to have hyper-focus, and may be unable to shift their attention to the next task; they are often inflexible when it comes to their routines, with low tolerance for change. Many are highly sensitive or insensitive to sensory input, like light, noise and touch, and may 'stim'. (source: *www.tiny.cc/Chadd*). See the chapter: *'S is for stimming'*. Autistic traits are said to be more 'stable' than those of ADHD behaviours, which show greater variability in their presentation. (Source: *www.tiny.cc/Yael_Leitner*). It would therefore be normal for someone diagnosed with both autism and ADHD to present completely differently on different days, and of course to feel very different on different days, depending on which 'condition' is dominant and what external factors are present (e.g. nutrition / sleep / sensory challenges). Both neurologies are said to affect the central nervous system, which is responsible for movement, language, memory, and social and focusing skills. (Source: *www.tiny.cc/Chadd*).

The two neurologies do have similar traits. A further comment from this author's familial experience would be that someone who is autistic and whose sensory system is under-stimulated may 'sensory seek' – e.g. run, climb, seek pressure, spin around – in order to recalibrate their body. This more energetic presentation of autism has similarities to ADHD traits. Some studies show that up to 50% of autists also manifest ADHD traits (particularly at pre-school age). Similarly, estimates suggest two-thirds of individuals with ADHD show features of autism (source: *www.tiny.cc/Yael_Leitner*). The issue in terms of diagnosis is that both autism and ADHD often include difficulties in attention, communication with peers, impulsivity, and various degrees of restlessness or hyperactivity. Both neurologies can cause significant behavioural, academic, emotional, and adaptive challenges in all settings. It is also worth noting that anxiety and mood disorders, although highly prevalent in autists, are said to be even more prevalent in individuals who have ADHD. (Source: *www.tiny.cc/GordonLipkin).*

However, in the author's personal opinion and familial experience, having both neurologies does not necessarily equate to twice the challenges. Maybe just a different set of challenges!

There are perhaps positives to be gleaned from having autism and ADHD, in terms of some of the restrictive and limiting elements of autism being potentially reduced at certain times, when the more impulsive and sociable elements of ADHD are dominant.

It is important to be upfront. It is proposed that there's a risk for 'increased severity of psycho-social problems' (depression and anxiety etc), with a dual diagnosis of autism and ADHD. (*www.tiny.cc/Yael_Leitner*). However, having an understanding about the two neurologies at an early age surely helps families and educators (and the autist themselves) to manage their challenges, in order to ward off such problems? (E.g. talking therapies like CBT, dietary support or management, and skills training to help cope with daily life, e.g. 'social skills' training via a child's school programme).

In a study on mood disorder (*www.tiny.cc/GordonLipkin*), it was reported that anxiety disorder and mood disorder, while very common in autistics, are even more common when children also have ADHD. Knowing in advance that anxiety and mood disorders are a big risk factor for autistic individuals with ADHD means interventions and supports can be given in advance, to help promote good mental health. Adaptions can hopefully be made, and demands can be reduced, in order to prevent anxiety in the individual. It is a good idea for the autist themselves to gain an understanding of their neurology, how they present on different days (e.g. which 'condition' is more dominant, and how that feels), and also what external factors (food, sleep etc) are contributory.

Age-appropriate medication to readdress neurotransmitter levels in individuals with ADHD may be suggested/prescribed; stimulants are the most common type of medication prescribed for ADHD and are believed to work by increasing dopamine levels in the brain, boosting concentration and reducing impulsive behaviours. However, medication is said to have the potential to be less effective for autistic individuals with ADHD, and may cause more side effects including social withdrawal and depression, as opposed to when the medications were used to treat ADHD alone. (Source: *www.tiny.cc/Chadd*). The National Institute for Health and Care Excellence (NICE) recommends that the first steps in treatment for ADHD for young people include help with behaviour and stress management, as well as educational support. (There is extensive advice on treatment and medication for ADHD at: *www.tiny.cc/NICE_adhd*).

So to answer the question of whether being autistic and having ADHD 'buffers' the two neurological sub-types to some degree, the author would have to collate extensive opinions of individuals with both neurologies in order to comment fairly. But in the author's familial experience, there's a possibility that the duality of austism and ADHD has the potential to provide some kind of 'buffering' effect, for example in terms of reducing extreme behaviours. As an example, this 'offsetting' element could perhaps be beneficial to an individual's safety; e.g. if the impulsivity of ADHD was offset somehow by a more rational and logical mindset. (An example is a child running into an unsafe area impulsively).

Again in the author's familial experience, a combined neurology of autism and ADHD could potentially mean that outsiders like educators and extended family members do not initially see that the behaviours of the person are atypical. E.g. a dual diagnosis of autism and ADHD could conceivably mean that the individual could present more like a neurotypical (NT or non-autistic) person, depending on their age. It doesn't mean they feel NT inside of course, or that their challenges are reduced –

just that the extremes (e.g. the restrictive and limiting elements of autism, versus the more impulsive and sociable elements of ADHD), somehow meet in the middle. Remember, no two autists are the same; we all experience life differently, and this is also true when co-existing conditions are present.

ADHD is a lifelong condition, however the characteristics may alter with age, e.g. the hyperactivity element is said to be much more common in children than in adults. Some adults report a large decrease in traits of ADHD as they age, however this could be due to their own management of their challenges. This reduction in overt signs leads some experts to propose that ADHD isn't lifelong; however the respected consensus is that ADHD does not go away.

Experts propose that a dual diagnosis of autism and ADHD potentially allows for more efficient clinical management of such individuals, and: *'Clears the way for a more precise scientific understanding of the overlap of these two disorders'* – (source: *www.tiny.cc/Yael_Leitner*). As we have described elsewhere, a neurodevelopmental diagnosis allows the individual to uniquely gain an understanding of their neurology, in a way that many NTs do not have – after all, anxiety and depression are prevalent across the wider population, e.g. across all neurologies. (See the chapter: *'A is for anxiety'*). This author believes that understanding one's own neurology, in the way that many autists do, is a benefit in terms of safeguarding mental health and knowing how to administer 'self-care'.

If any parent or educator is concerned that a child is exhibiting disproportionate levels of anxiety, plus a kind of 'double-sided personality' with extremes of mood, as well as the usual signs of autism like social and communicative issues, repetitive behaviours and sensory challenges, and signs of ADHD such as impulsivity and lack of focus, it may be worth investigating the possibility of a co-existing ADHD diagnosis too, with the relevant clinician.

The autist's view

It is encouraging that more clinicians have the experience to diagnose the two neurologies together. I can't speak personally, as I don't have ADHD (although I have autistic family members who also have ADHD), but I can only imagine, as an autist, how challenging being autistic and also having ADHD must be. Especially for children, who are navigating a confusing world as it is, without the extra neurodevelopmental challenges. I do believe that the 'buffering' effect of the two neurologies could be true, so would urge parents whose children may have autism and ADHD to consider the positive elements of a dual diagnosis, e.g. that the limiting elements of autism may be coerced out by the more sociable elements of ADHD, and the impulsive elements of ADHD may be reined in by autism's restrictive tendencies.

B is for
black and white thinking

Autists are renowned for their black and white thinking styles. While we will start here by detailing the challenges this brings, at the end of this chapter, we have detailed some information on the benefits of black and white thinking. Also described as polarised or inflexible thinking, black and white thinking, a phenomenon that's not limited to autists, is usually linked to negativity. (In that the negative voice common in this thinking style may overwhelm us, e.g.: *I'm a failure, he/she hates me, I am no good at reading*', etc).

Experts agree that black and white thinking is caused by heightened levels of emotional arousal to everyday situations. It is usually earmarked by immediacy and impulsivity. This thinking style is a limiting factor for autists and, when linked to impulsivity, can lead to knee-jerk decisions that are not helpful; examples include breaking off a friendship after a small dis-agreement, or abandoning a hobby due to an ill-perceived sense of failure, or overt perfectionism. However, despite being a naturally occurring thinking style for many autists, it is perfectly possible to adapt and limit negative black and white thinking. (Although to what degree various enormously, depending on the individual and many other factors, notably any mental health issues and other co-existing conditions). This 'greyness' is seemingly easier to achieve as an adult, however young autists can also be taught to question their thinking styles. Key points in terms of trying to change a repetitive, negative thought pattern, or an 'all or nothing' approach, would be:

* Helping the child to look for evidence to back up the thought; e.g. 'Am I really no good at art? This drawing isn't my best work, but I have painted beautiful pictures before'. Or, 'Is my friendship with 'X' really over? Or was this a small disagreement that's part of the fabric of our relationship?'

* Finding perspective can help too, especially in terms of blame. Yes, person 'X' threw the punch; but what happened previously, and were they provoked?

* Developing choices. It's easy as a black and white thinker to sometimes feel that stopping, leaving, abandoning and walking away is the only real option. One useful tool, especially for children, is to remember there are always other options – and that this abandonment option is usually option B. We can help young autists gain perspective by working out what the 'A' choice could be. It may seem harder, but it has more potential benefits. E.g. stay for ten minutes, as we could discover a great new skill, or gain a prize? Or try the new menu, in case we discover a new favourite taste? Sometimes, waiting and looking for the evidence helps us make a good choice. For example, a child doesn't want to enter the room of a birthday party, saying they're too tired, or feel ill – in all likelihood, they're anxious, as the excursion is out of their comfort zone of 'sameness'. Going home is the B option – but what is the evidence for feeling tired or ill? Is their body tricking them? Could waiting for a few minutes outside help them look at their choices? Maybe option A could involve the birthday child coming outside to say hello; or the worried child entering the room for ten

minutes and sitting with the parent, to count the balloons? If they then decide they want to leave, this is ok of course, but some 'thinking time' helps with the issue of immediacy, linked to impulsivity. As many autists respond well to visual cues, a traffic light graphic could help with choice-making. If red is option B, amber is thinking time, and green is option A, this may help autists look for (and wait for) other options and perspectives.

* Another idea when trying to change a repetitive, negative thought pattern is to scale one's feelings from 1-10, with ten being the worst. How much of a failure was the issue? Did I just not reach a personal best, but still made an average score? (What did everyone else score; again, seeking evidence). If today's occurrence scored an eight, what other occurrences scored an eight recently, and what was the outcome? Did they stay an eight, or could I lower the number, on reflection?

* Keeping an actual chart and writing the details down can help too, especially if it involves tracking emotions; e.g. 'That class was awful, I felt too embarrassed', and giving the experience a five. Next time, if you repeat the exercise and score a four, the evidence shows you that your skill-sets (or those of a child you're working with) have improved.

Let's now move onto the positives of black and white thinking. Whilst black and white thinking is undoubtedly unhelpful for the most part, there are some positives! Here are ten ways that autists may have positive skill-sets, due to their inflexible thinking styles:

* Cutting to the chase in business – removing the irrelevant data, and seeing the important elements. (If

something's good or bad, or right or wrong, decisions can be made more quickly).

* Not getting caught up in the emotionally-draining dramas that many neurotypical (NT) individuals can sometimes become embroiled in; e.g. who said what to who, etc. This lack of importance attributed to trivial matters often leads to good, logical problem solving.

* Sticking to rules that help us – in terms of safety and security, health and wellness, legality, etc. Right and wrong thinking styles can help us stay safe.

* Generating action in a business capacity – less endless meetings, boardroom discussions, and pros and cons charts – logic is applied, and a decision is made. Simple.

* Sorting the available data to find a problem – this could be why something doesn't add up, why a part has malfunctioned, or why a machine doesn't perform well. Not paying attention to the grey or inconsequential information helps the individual solve a problem efficiently.

* Expertise – autists are known for developing special interests and even obsessing about certain elements – together with black and white thinking, this helps them see a way to reach a goal logically. These combined factors mean autists often excel in key areas of sport, technology or the creative fields, because their heightened interests mean they're often open to practice and repetition, and ultimately, expertise.

* Good employees – autists are renowned as being loyal and dedicated employees, due to a leaning towards rule-keeping. This can involve punctuality, reliability and honesty; all valuable workplace skills.

* Great pattern recognition, due to the brain ignoring the unnecessary grey areas – useful for memory, and learning techniques that require repetition.

* Attention to detail – again, in business, this can be beneficial for highly technical roles involving data. Honing in on what's important helps the autist see areas that their NT peers may miss. It also reduces the risk of 'mis-remembering' information. And sometimes the little elements make all the difference. Attention to detail is also a good skill to have in everyday life.

* Loyal and trusting natures – this often makes autists good friends and romantic partners. Whilst autists may of course have challenges in relationships, especially relating to some areas of communication, they are often the shoulder to cry on, the reliable friend who keeps appointments, the individual that can solve a problem and see a way through a crisis, the partner who arrives for a date on time, and the person who upholds the values of monogamy and shared couple values.

The autist's view

Black and white thinking can be very challenging. If you're an undiagnosed autist, you may not even realise you're doing it – you may believe the voice in your head, e.g. the one described previously as stating things like: 'I'm a failure, he/she hates me, I am no good at reading'.

However, this author has a further good tip, gleaned from Phil Parker's Lightning Process training, which I undertook. (The Lightning Process attempts to modify the brain's thought patterns to reduce stress-related hormones, and was designed by British osteopath Phil Parker in the late 1990s – visit: *www.lightningprocess.com*). The tip is to remind oneself of what you are doing or feeling in the moment, or the hour, or the day. Black and white thinking makes us think in extremes (e.g. 'I will never lose weight, I can't give up this addictive habit, I will never feel well again', etc). But framing the issue as something we are doing at the moment, rather than something that we will necessarily also be doing tomorrow, next week or later today, helps give us some perspective. It can be very hard when parenting a child with rigidity of thinking, as they often cannot be coerced into trying something new, going somewhere that you know they will enjoy, or continuing with a sport or activity that you know they're good at. However, developing A and B choices and seeking evidence for what they're feeling can help them develop an awareness of their own thought processes.

B is for burnout

Do you know the phrase 'burning the candle at both ends'? Autistic burnout, in this author's opinion and experience, is when your candle has burned out – a physiological symptom of system overload. If autistic shutdown (see the chapter: '*S is for shutdown*') is more of a short-term self-preservation mode from a mental and emotional perspective (when you need to start closing down some of the metaphorical mental browsers, apps and programmes in your brain, to conserve emotional energy), burnout is the next, physiological step.

Burnout can occur when the candle is being burned at both ends without enough replenishment to counteract the areas in which the autistic individual struggles, or uses up the most energy units – e.g. social, communication and sensory. Everyone, no matter what their neurology, experiences low mood and tiredness, and potentially has the capability to burn out – but autistic burnout is slightly different, in that it usually relates to the autist's individual challenges.

Let's look at the energy depletion caused by masking. The autist (especially, it seems, if female), tends to use up a lot of energy on 'autistic masking', or fitting in (you can read more about energy exertion in the chapter: '*H is for hangover (social)*', which includes information on the spoons theory; and also in the chapter '*M is for masking*'). Most autists face some kind of difficulty with fitting in, especially if they are undiagnosed and unaware of their autism, or if they are young and still getting to know the various social conventions. Avoiding autistic burnout probably only becomes easier once you know what self-care tools you need in your emotional toolbox, and once you know more about your own functioning fluctuations, or your 'spectrum within a spectrum' – see the chapter: '*K is for knowing your own spectrum*').

Going back to the issue of masking as a factor for burnout; what would be classed as 'fitting in'? Maybe engaging in expected conversation at work, appearing unperturbed by sensory difficulties when shopping, and managing the challenges of certain socialisations, e.g. extended family get-togethers or office parties. This 'masking' is often required in order to hold down a job, access education services or maintain relationships, and can be an automatic reflex, rather than something calculated. However, the processing power and social energy required to maintain the mask can be very depleting.

Blogger Ryan Boren writes eloquently about autistic burnout as follows – "*Periods of burnout caused problems at school and work. I would lose executive function and self-care skills. My capacity for sensory and social overload dwindled to near nothing. I avoided speaking and retreated from socializing. I was spent. I couldn't maintain the facade anymore. I had to stop and pay the price.*" (Source: *www.tiny.cc/RyanBoren*).

What tends to happen to autists who are responsible for others is that this important element continues to function during burnout – e.g. their duties as a parent or carer – but other everyday functions have to be 'turned off'. In burnout, communication may deplete, sensory overload is common, self-care skills (perhaps including seemingly simple things, like taking care of one's appearance) become of less importance – essentially, this metaphorical computer's operating system is shutting down, so only the essential tasks remain 'on'. In autistic burnout, the individual may become withdrawn, their voice may become more monotone due to the sheer effort of communicating (some autists may even become non-verbal), and they are likely to be very sensitive to sensory input. Many autists experience anxiety, symptoms of low mood, dysthymia or depression during their lives, and during burnout, these conditions could well resurface.

(Greta Thunberg, the climate activist, previously experienced depression and issues with eating, in what could represent autistic burnout. In her TED Talk (see: *www.tinycc/Greta_T*), she explained how, at the age of eleven, several years after learning about the concept of climate change for the first time, she fell into a depression and became ill. *"I stopped talking. I stopped eating. In two months, I lost about ten kilos of weight. Later on I was diagnosed with Asperger's Syndrome, OCD, and selective mutism; that basically means I only speak when I think it's necessary,"* she described. Greta may or may not have been in 'burnout', however depression and changes in vocalisation are common in individuals experiencing this state.

Autistic burnout as a state may last a matter of weeks, or perhaps a couple of months, and it can be cyclical – a regular (if not frequent) occurrence. Anyone in more longer-term burnout than this would likely need a great deal of support in their lives, to become strong and well again. (Total burnout can be linked to some kind of large-scale life milestone, or occurrence – the individual would likely not be able to continue to go to work, or stay their place of education, until they recover sufficiently. This author has heard multiple stories of autistic pre-teens having to drop out of the school environment due to a lack of coping mechanisms, skillsets or support, and needing to recalibrate emotionally, and become well again).

So here's this author's take on autistic burnout. Treat lower level autistic burnout as something akin to a migraine. Would we expect someone with a migraine to go to work, merrily do the shopping, look their best, and casually chat about trivia? No, they would likely head to bed, and rest. They have reduced functionality at that moment in time, and need to recuperate. To emphasise – burnout is a physiological symptom of system overload. The individual generally needs time to recuperate in a low-demand environment, with as few challenges in the areas of communication, sensory triggers and socialisation as is possible. In serious cases, the individual would likely not be able to continue to go to work or school, for a time at least; and maybe longer term.

This author sees burnout as a more drastic example of shutdown. (See the chapter: 'S is for shutdown'). Autistic burnout may however be avoided by knowing yourself (as an autist), knowing what triggers you, how often you must rest or have social downtime, reducing social activities when you're feeling sensitive, using self-care tools like headphone time when you need to recalibrate.... and removing things or people from your life that deplete your 'energy bank', rather than fill it up. Aspects like sleep and nutrition also undoubtedly play a part, e.g. poor sleep and nutrition may exacerbate the low moods and tiredness. As Ryan Boren found: "I was spent. I had to stop."

In children who don't yet have this level of self-awareness, reducing demands, allowing the child choices in their decision making, reducing socialisation and sensory triggers, and generally allowing rest or down time could be beneficial. (With liaison with their educators, if appropriate). Individuals in more severe stages of burnout could need all of the above, as well as perhaps talking therapies, health and nutritional support, and the support of any education or work places, to allow the autist to recover and plan any return. Obviously, support from the individual's GP or other relevant healthcare provider should also be sought if the individual's condition is serious.

The autist's view

I believe I experienced burnout in my teens, when my GP diagnosed Myalgic Encephalomyelitis (M.E)., a chronic condition that causes symptoms affecting the nervous and immune systems. I experienced debilitating fatigue for many years, and my body and brain seemingly had an inability to recover after expending even small amounts of energy. In the chapter: 'K *is for knowing your own spectrum*', I describe how tracking your energy levels and functionality challenges can help prevent shutdown or burnout, in my opinion.

C is for
co-existing conditions

This chapter is probably one of the most important, in terms of the modern way of looking at autism embraced by fans of the neurodiversity paradigm (see the chapter: *'N is for neurodiversity'*). E.g. considering autism to be intrinsically a difference in processing, with other debilitating or co-existing medical conditions being additions to the autism, not part of the autism. Please be reminded that this author does not propose to be a medical expert, and that individuals should always seek the care of a qualified doctor or relevant healthcare professional to discuss their own personal healthcare status, or that of their families.

A recent American study (source: *www.tiny.cc/GNSoke*) looked at the prevalence of co-occurring conditions in autistic children, finding that the eight-year-olds in the study had an average of 4.9 co-existing or co-occurring conditions, and 98% of them had at least one co-occurring condition. The four-year-olds in the study had an average of 3.8 co-occurring conditions; 96% of them had at least one. Interestingly, the condition that is perhaps most associated with autism as a public perception, cognitive developmental disability, (a term that encompasses intellectual disability, and also disabilities that can affect cognitive and physical functioning), was present in just 15.6% of the autistic children in the study. This resource puts the prevalence of co-existing conditions to autism at a higher rate that most sources quote. Generally, it is cited that around seventy percent of autistic children are thought to have an additional medical or psychiatric condition (source: *www.tiny.cc/simonoff*). This occurrence is diagnostically called 'co-morbidity'. The common co-existing conditions associated with autism can be at the very least debilitating, and in many cases, considerably life-changing. It is important to note that this book is in no way a medical tome; anyone seeking to learn more about the conditions detailed here should seek further clarification from relevant, expert sources. However, the author has detailed below some of the most common co-existing conditions to autism, fantastically described by writer Maxfield Sparrow, writing for the Thinking Autism Guide (see: *www.tiny.cc/MaxfieldSparrow*), as '*genetic hitchhikers that love to travel with autism*'.

Anxiety disorders

Some studies indicate that up to 84% of autistic individuals have some form of anxiety (source: *www.tiny.cc/v_Postorino*). Another study in young people found that 39% of autistic adolescents had criteria for 'a lifetime history of an anxiety disorder' (source: *www.tiny.cc/mazefsky*).

Anxiety might show up in autistic children in a variety of ways, e.g. stimming more often (see the chapter: '*S is for stimming*'), asking questions repeatedly or fixating on something, withdrawing emotionally, deliberately hurting themselves, having trouble getting to sleep, or experiencing meltdowns (see the chapter: '*M is for meltdowns*').

A well-known anxiety disorder is Obsessive Compulsive Disorder (OCD); people with OCD behave in repetitive and compulsive ways. Around 17% of autists (of all ages) may have OCD, according to one study (source: *www.tiny.cc/steensel*).

Other estimates state that the number of children and adolescent autists who also have OCD could be as high as 37%. (Source: *www.tiny.cc/v_Postorino*).

The overlap between OCD and autism is still unclear; both groups may experience unusual responses to sensory experiences, while OCD's compulsions can resemble the 'insistence on sameness' or repetitive behaviours that many autists also experience.

In general, it is thought that psychiatric disorders are common in many autists. The aforementioned study on autism and co-existing conditions (*www.tiny.cc/simonoff*) states that: *'Psychiatric disorders are common and frequently multiple in children with autism spectrum disorders. Co-morbid conditions can appear at any time during a child's development. Some might not appear until later in adolescence or adulthood. Sometimes these co-morbid conditions have symptoms that affect how well autism spectrum disorder therapies and interventions work.'*

Attention Deficit Hyperactivity Disorder (ADHD)

According to the National Autistic Society (NAS), ADHD is common in autistic individuals. The NAS asked experts from the South London and Maudsley Hospital to explain how ADHD can affect children and adults, and the article may be found at the NAS website: *www.autism.org.uk*. The experts stated that while autism and ADHD share some common characteristics, like not seeming to listen when people speak, interrupting, or intruding on other people's personal space, if someone has ADHD, they predominantly struggle with impulsivity, hyperactivity and inattention. Often, children with ADHD have difficulty focusing on one activity or task; they may be easily distracted, and they are often physically unable to sit still. As with autism, children with ADHD often have difficulty moving their attention to other activities, when they are asked to do so. (Source: *www.tiny.cc/Chadd*). Please also see the chapter: '*A is for autism and ADHD*', for more information on a dual diagnosis of autism and ADHD (or a diagnosis of autism, with ADHD as a co-morbidity).

Depression and dysthymia

Studies definitively link depressive symptoms with autism. One study examined the potential relationship between co-existing depression or anxiety in adolescents with (as was then described as) 'high-functioning ASD', and found that 32% of autistic adolescents met criteria for '*A lifetime history of a co-morbid depressive disorder*'. (Source: *www.tiny.cc/mazefsky*). Likely linked to the individual's constant struggle to 'process' and socialise in a neurotypical world, depressive symptoms like low mood, lack of motivation, trouble sleeping and poor appetite are common signs in autists. An interesting research document (source: *www.tiny.cc/Dheeraj_Rai*) states: '*[In studies], individuals with ASDs, especially those without intellectual disability, had a greater risk of a depression diagnosis in young adulthood than the general population and their non-autistic siblings.*')

Dysthymia, also known as Dysthymic Disorder or Persistent depressive disorder (PDD), is a relatively little-known condition of chronic depression. It is characterised as a chronic low-grade depression, persistent irritability, and a state of demoralisation, often with low self-esteem. However there's little information available regarding its prevalence with autism. Purely anecdotally though, from this author's point of view and with limited peer-group research, it does seem to be fairly common in autistic individuals.

Fragile X Syndrome

Fragile X is a genetic disorder and intellectual disability; the syndrome is said to be the most common inherited cause of intellectual disability, and children with the condition have difficulty communicating. Autism is common in children with Fragile X, so autism can be described as a co-existing condition of Fragile X. (You can read more about it at the Fragile X Society's website: *www.fragilex.org.uk*). It has been proposed by some individuals that Fragile X Syndrome is the most common genetic cause of autism, accounting for approximately 5% of cases. (Source: *www.tiny.cc/Fragilex*).

Gastrointestinal symptoms

Common gastrointestinal symptoms for autistic people reportedly include constipation, abdominal pain, diarrhoea and stomach bloating. (Source: *www.tiny.cc/chaidez*). There's also an increasing amount of research on a proposed gut-brain connection in people of all neurologies (source: *www.tiny.cc/harvard-health*). Various studies have looked at GI dysfunction in autistic individuals; however, sources proposing that autism and so-called 'symptoms' are the result of gut issues are (to date) unsubstantiated. Such links even lead to disturbing practices that harm autists. The National Institute for Health and Care Excellence (NICE) advises parents and carers not to subject autistic individuals to any exclusion diets, in order to 'manage autistic symptoms'. The UK's National Health Service (NHS) advises: 'There are no treatments or cures for autism itself. Special diets – such as gluten-free, casein-free or ketogenic - can be harmful.'

Intellectual disability and developmental delays / disabilities

The NAS puts the number of autistic individuals with co-existing, intellectual disabilities, e.g. disorders characterised by a limited mental capacity and difficulty with adaptive behaviours such as social interactions, at between 44-52%; around half of all autists. The incorrect pre-conception that all autists are intellectually challenged is something that autists face consistently. As mentioned, one American study (source: *www.tiny.cc/GNSoke*) found that 'cognitive developmental disability', a term that encompasses cognitive functioning and intellectual disability, was present in just 15.6% of the autistic children in the study.

Incidentally, there is always confusion to be found when writing about such terms, as British writers sometimes use the term 'learning disability' in this context to mean intellectual disabilities and below-average IQ, as well as the literal meaning of challenges in learning, e.g. weaknesses in academic skills. The UK's NHS describes intellectual disability as: *'A group of disorders characterised by a limited mental capacity and difficulty with adaptive behaviours such as social interactions'.* They describe developmental disability as: *'A severe, long term disability that can affect cognitive ability, physical functioning, or both. The term 'developmental disability' encompasses intellectual disability but also includes physical disabilities'.* See: *www.tiny.cc/DefinitionDisabilities*).

One clinical analysis (*www.tiny.cc/Sappok*) describes intellectual disability as being: *'Diagnosed when a child who is six years or older and has an IQ below 70, as well as difficulties with daily tasks. In children under six years, the term 'developmental delay' is used when children have significant cognitive and language delays.'* In terms of the prevalence of intellectual disability, figures vary according to territory, however about 1% of the general population is thought to have an intellectual disability; meanwhile, about 10% of individuals with intellectual disability are thought to be autistic or have autistic traits. (Source: *www.tiny.cc/ASrivastava*). Interestingly, since America's Centers for Disease Control (CDC) has been measuring prevalence rates of autism and co-occurring intellectual disability, the rate of autistic individuals who do not have co-occurring intellectual disability has been rising. E.g. there are reportedly now more autistic individuals without intellectual disability being diagnosed in the USA.

Apraxia of speech

As we cited in the first chapter, co-existing conditions associated with autism can affect communication in various ways – some autists are non-verbal, with apraxia of speech. However, research continues on the subject of whether this is a true co-existing condition, or a result of autists' 'social reciprocity challenges', e.g. somehow part of the autism itself, stemming from a difference in the structure of that individual's temporal lobe, the area of the brain involved in auditory perception (source: *www.tiny.cc/SpeechApraxia*). It is important to note that a speech difference or lack of speech is not necessarily an indicator of intellectual ability, as the many non-verbal autistic writers, bloggers and vloggers (e.g. Carly Fleischmann, Ido Kedar and Naoki Higashida,) who are sharing their stories online and in books, are proving. Just because one can't speak, surely does not mean one is not articulate and intelligent?

Anorexia nervosa

Anorexia nervosa is not currently widely considered to be a common co-existing condition of autism. But should it be? The latest research certainly pinpoints a link. The charity Autistica said 'findings' suggest one in five women presenting to UK clinics with anorexia may also be autistic (sharing the information available at *www.tiny.cc/Anorexia*); health watchdog the National Institute for Health and Clinical Excellence (NICE) conservatively said in response that more research is required. It is proposed that some autists may develop anorexia due to autism's propensity for rigidity and hyper-focus, e.g. developing a set of rules about calorie intake. Autistica's director of science, Dr James Cusack, recently called for new guidelines from NICE. The two conditions have been researched over the years. The resource: *'Autism Spectrum Disorder in Anorexia Nervosa: An Updated Literature Review'* includes the main study resources (*www.tiny.cc/Anorexia-Nervosa*). The 'Current Psychiatry Reports' resource at this link finds that: *'Studies consistently report over-representation of symptoms of autism spectrum disorder (ASD) in AN [individuals with anorexia nervosa]. Co-morbid AN and ASD may require more intensive treatment or specifically tailored interventions.'*

The resource Spectrum News reports that: *'People with anorexia often have difficulties making friends and sustaining social relationships even before the onset of their condition. Because high levels of social discomfort and withdrawal persist even after they begin eating regularly and return to a normal weight, these social difficulties are not likely to have been caused by anorexia or malnutrition.'* (Source: *www.tiny.cc/AutismAN*).

Other co-existing conditions associated with autism, including epilepsy

There are a number of other co-existing conditions associated with autism that include Tourette Syndrome, Dyslexia, Dyspraxia, and Downs Syndrome – but due to the constraints of this book, the author refers readers to other resources, for further reading on these conditions – please do check out the websites of: Synapse Australia – (see: *www.tiny.cc/synapse-Comorbid);* and also the resource: Common Neurological Comorbidities in ASDs, from 'Current Opinion in Pediatrics' – (see: *www.tiny.cc/Comorbidities).*

Epilepsy is also a serious co-existing factor for autists, and is seriously implicated in mortality rates for autists. (See: *www.tiny.cc/mortality-ASD).* The Epilepsy Foundation (see: *www.epilepsy.com)* states that there is an association between epilepsy and autism, in that children with autism are a little more likely to have epilepsy, while children with epilepsy are a little more likely to have autism. However, as this book is in no way a medical tome, the author will refer interested individuals to research the links themselves. (The National Autistic Society, which describes 'a strong association between epilepsy, intellectual disability and autism', has useful information at its website: *www.autism.org.uk).*

The autist's view

As we have seen, many autists experience co-existing conditions – over the years, mine have been gastrointestinal symptoms, mild anxiety and dysthymia. As discussed in the: '*A is for anxiety*' chapter, as an (undiagnosed autistic) child, I experienced several anxiety-related issues, including episodes of hyperventilation and a recurring metabolic condition that was probably linked to the excessive release of stress hormones. This metabolic condition occurred at least once a year for the entire duration of my school years. (Mysteriously stopping after I left school!) However, once I entered the workplace, a new anxiety-linked condition appeared, irritable bowel syndrome; a common gastrointestinal condition. Again, this occurred consistently while I was in the workplace, mysteriously disappearing once I started working for myself! It is clear now that stress and anxiety played a major factor in these conditions, but now I have the awareness and skillsets to manage (and prevent) them.

Dysthymia, a chronic low-grade depression, is also something I have experienced, and consider to be part of my neurology. Once a counsellor explained it to me, it became something I didn't need to be too concerned about – it is not something that needs to be fixed, in my case. It is a symptom of my neurology, and the stresses I face daily as an autist; a gentle reminder not to over-do it, in life. I take a natural dietary supplement that I believe helps with low-mood and anxiety, and I try to pay close attention to emotional self-care, to keep the dysthymia in check. Obviously, there are a number of much more serious co-existing conditions affecting autists which can be really debilitating and life-changing, and the links between all of the conditions are constantly being researched.

C is for communication

This chapter will explore the issues surrounding communication as an autistic individual. It is important to remember that it takes two to tango, and it takes two to converse; we will discuss this concept further into the chapter. Let's firstly imagine a scenario. There is a mum in the school playground, and she seems a little different – you could say she is quirky.

There are a few small visual differences – maybe she has cool, coloured hair, the odd piercing or tattoo, and isn't following the fashion sense of most of the mums; there's an air of quietness about her that makes her seem aloof. But that's not unusual, right? Lots of people have body adornments, and don't follow the fashion pack; and many of us are introverted. But it's not just that there's something slightly different about her appearance and body language, when compared to most of the other parents and the adults at the school. Her gaze and eyeline are somewhat irregular, and her conversation is peppered with unusual timings of the expressive gestures of the hands and face. All subtle differences, but there, none the less.

There's a further difference, however. A difference in terms of How People Interact With Her. The fact that she is autistic, and the other neurotypical (NT) adults know she's somehow different even before she speaks, is apparently 'to be expected', and normal – human nature. It has been proposed that NT people subconsciously know that an autistic individual is different, and respond accordingly, usually in a subconscious manner. (Read more at: *www.tiny.cc/ASD-communication*). An unusual facial expression, a pause in the beat of conversation (or no pause when one is expected), a relaxed face instead of a smile, a perceived-aloof demeanour – any number of tiny subtle differences that a psychologist may notice (but that untrained eyes do not), mark this woman in our example out as being slightly different.

The ostracism that autistic individuals experience is not necessarily a conscious process – it happens intrinsically, like a sort of miscommunication at the most raw level. If the woman in our example does not know she is autistic, she may well develop feelings of low mood affecting her confidence, and may experience feelings of loneliness, rejection and other issues like depression. She may even style her body differently, in terms of adornments or hair colour, just to pre-empt other people's perceptions of her, or create a kind of barrier or field around her – again, this may be subconscious, almost like another level of autistic masking. (See the chapter: *'M is for masking'*). She is aware of the dismissive behaviour of many of her peers, workmates and associates. In any case, she may not wish to fit it with the in-crowd of alpha females she often encounters. But she's spent years being a people pleaser, so probably keeps on trying to make the effort to be approachable at some level. (It should be noted of course that any 'dismissive' behaviour shown toward the autist could itself be caused by the third party's own insecurities, neurological differences or social difficulties!)

Not everyone blanks the autistic woman in our example, of course. The mums that have taken the time to have a conversation now know her a little better; and there are always the other neurodivergent types and fellow autistics that she fits in with, as well as people seemingly attuned to the more sensitive mind.

Communication is clearly a two-way thing. According to expert lecturers like Dr. Damian Milton and Dr. Luke Beardon, a concept called 'the double empathy problem' helps clarify why, when people with different experiences of the world interact, they may struggle to connect. Some current studies, such as that by University of Edinburgh researcher Dr. Catherine Crompton (source: *www.tiny.cc/Crompton*), concur, showing that NT people may be less willing to interact socially with autistic people.

These particular study results suggest that this lack of connection is more apparent when autists are interacting with NT people, and that the 'miscommunication' is alleviated when there are interactions between two autistic people. It seems we're all more comfortable when conversing with our own neurotype. Using this framework to look at autists' so-called 'emotional reciprocity', we can see that the so-called deficits in non-verbal communication (that have become central to autism discussions), are integral to the second party.

But to what extent do specific personality or neurology types make a difference? Is it fair to assume that most of the communication difficulties occur between an autist and an NT individual? Or more specifically, between an autist and a non-empathic, or more impatient NT individual? Autists are often drawn to other autists, or 'sensitive' types – and this can be seen at pre-school age in children, even if verbal conversation isn't a factor. It is usually a subconscious 'attraction'; and not just in the romantic sense. Here's another scenario to illustrate that it takes two to tango, and two to converse. What if a Japanese person met someone fluent in the little spoken Creole language, Taki-Taki, from South America? Would we automatically blame the South American for the difficulty in mutual communication? That would be foolish, as both individuals would struggle, based on what is known to them linguistically, and their communication abilities at that time. The report that has been referenced earlier in the chapter states that many aspects of social presentation are 'atypical' in autistic individuals, including abnormal facial expressivity, irregular use of gaze, lower rates (or unusual timing) of expressive gestures, and unusual speech patterns. The report concludes: *'The reluctance of 'typically developing' individuals to engage in social interactions with their autism spectrum disorder [ASD] peers further limits the opportunities for individuals with ASD to practice their already fragile social skills. This can have a significant negative impact on the ability of socially aware and socially interested individuals with ASD to improve their social communication abilities.'*

This author's conclusion? Autists aren't failing at communication. We don't need to beat ourselves up for perceived social faux pas. We're simply communicating in the way our autism allows us to communicate. Just as the NT individuals who don't always engage with us are doing what comes naturally to them! Importantly, it is not the autist's fault. We just see the world a little differently, and communicate in subtly different ways.

Moving onto to another area of communication concerning autists: many clinicians advocate choosing language wisely when communicating with autistic children, using both non-verbal and verbal communication. As we know, communication difficulties are a big factor for autists – some autists communicate verbally, some don't; and some experience selective mutism, which the UK's NHS defines as occurring when: *'The expectation to talk to certain people triggers a freeze response, with feelings of panic, rather like a bad case of stage fright; talking is impossible.'* Verbalisation isn't the only way to communicate of course – and in today's high-tech world, there is an array of communication systems (e.g. the Picture Exchange Communication System or PECS, which utilises pictures for visual support, in order to develop communication and social skills), as well as various computer and tablet devices and 'apps' that allow non-verbal individuals to communicate.

So, as mentioned, many clinicians advocate using both non-verbal and verbal communication when interacting with autistic children. It is important to remember that autists (of any age) are easily 'overloaded' – through the experiences of their day, the surrounding environment, and any number of factors that have consumed their 'emotional bandwidth' on that day, or at that time. Talking at length with them, and talking at all sometimes, can be an extra drain on their bandwidth and resources. Hence, using non-verbal communication can be useful. Read more about this below, under *'The autist's view'*. Please also see the chapter: *'X is for expressive and receptive language'*, which goes into more detail regarding communication via speech.

The autist's view

As detailed above, many clinicians advocate using both non-verbal and verbal communication when interacting with autistic children, which I also advocate. For example: just smiling as a welcome, to show your intentions are positive; giving a thumbs up, which could actually serve the purpose of the question: 'Are you OK'?, e.g. if the autistic individual wasn't able to talk in the moment, perhaps as they were too upset. Also, averting eye contact, if the autist finds it uncomfortable.

Other non-verbal communications include signing (e.g. British or American Sign Language, and Makaton – I wrote a book for babies and young children called 'Alfie's Magic Hat: Fun At The Zoo', which utilises these signing methods, and is widely available online. Signing, once learned, can be incredibly useful for the autist and their family members, to help communicate when any family member is tired or overloaded). Other examples of non-verbal communication include utilising pictures, drawings and symbol charts in the course of communication, perhaps in a 'now and next' capacity, to help children understand the order of things that are happening, thus potentially lowering any anxieties related to uncertainty. Visual timetables are great, like a picture-based calendar, and the child can help create them, and make them colourful. Another example of useful non-verbal communication would be modelling a useful communication behaviour, such as nodding – e.g. '[Name of child], would you like toast and jam for breakfast?', and nodding yourself as you ask.

Examples of verbal communication that could help a young autist's understanding could include: using their name at the start of what you're saying, to aid focus; also, saying '[name of child], can I ask you a question?', before asking it, may gain their attention. Being specific with any questions, and not asking multiple questions in one sentence, can be beneficial. A tip I have found useful is to ask the neurodivergent child for help if you would like something done at home; e.g. rather than saying: 'Can you tidy the room please?', it could be, 'I'd love some help putting the toys away.' Equally, stating a fact can be useful, e.g. rather than saying: 'Can you tidy the room please?' (which after several times of asking can easily include a frustrated or irritated tone of voice!), 'Goodness, this room is messy!', is less confrontational.

Moving onto the issue of communication, and to what extent specific personality or neurology types make a difference where conversing is concerned, I do believe that autists are often drawn to other autists. And if the third party, e.g. the friend of an autist, isn't neurodivergent themselves, there's usually a good chance that their personality traits include empathy and patience towards atypical individuals. Very often, there are autistic individuals or other neurominorities in the third party's family, and their spouses may even be neurodivergent – this theory is just something I have observed within the autistic community who share their experiences online, and it also mirrors my own experiences.

D is for diagnosis

The route to autism diagnosis differs for every individual, and in the case of a child's assessment, a number of health professionals may be involved; see below. As readers will see within the chapter: *'R is for rights'*, autism assessment for children in the UK is legislated by the Children and Families Act 2014 – this aims to ensure increased protection for minors, including those with 'additional needs'. It advises local authorities to meet 'best practice' by developing an Autism Health Care Pathway, and produce legally binding Educational & Health Care Plans (EHCPs) for minors. (Please note that readers should consult their family doctor, their child's school representatives, and any local authority or service provider contacts, for details on autism diagnosis pathways / services in their locality / territory. The information shared here is correct at the time of writing.)

In the UK, the National Institute for Health and Care Excellence (NICE) lays down the guidelines for autism assessment that local authorities and health and social care commissioners should follow – (see: *www.tiny.cc/NICEpathway)*. For children requiring autism assessment, Local Authorities tend to refer individuals to the Community Paediatrics team, local specialist services, depending on the need, or the Child and Adolescent Mental Health Service, or CAMHS (although this service does have 'referral thresholds' that may include 'associated mental health difficulties').

Health professionals involved in autism diagnosis may include behaviour support teams or local inclusion teams (which may include school and nursery / pre-school teachers and staff, speech therapists and educational psychologists), general practitioners (GPs), CAMHS representatives, counsellors, psychotherapists, health visitors, occupational therapists, paediatricians, psychiatrists, special educational needs co-ordinators (SENCOs), social workers, care managers, and speech and language therapists. After referral by the relevant individual, autism assessments are commonly carried out for children by a multidisciplinary team lead by a paediatrician, e.g. a medical practitioner specialising in children (although some autism assessments may be carried out by a single practitioner, e.g. a neurodevelopmental paediatrician). With so many autistic children presenting with complex autism profiles, working with a paediatrician who has extensive experience in the field, for example someone describing themselves as a neurodevelopmental paediatrician, neuro-disability paediatrician or developmental-behavioural paediatrician, can be beneficial for families. Referrals for assessment are commonly made by GPs or school SENCOs, although other professionals as described above may also flag up concerns, and advise the best route to assessment.

Psychiatrists and clinical psychologists / neuro-psychologists / counselling psychologists commonly diagnose autism in adults. All diagnosing clinicians (for patients of all ages) use behavioural evaluations, which include clinical observations, the consideration of any medical history, as well as developmental tests. The autism diagnostic observation schedule (ADOS), a standardised assessment, is commonly used along with other evaluations. The duration of the assessment varies, but typically takes less than a morning. In the UK, autism assessments may be made via the NHS route, or privately.

Assessments are generally informal; nothing like an exam or test, and for children, they (should be!) made to feel fun, with ample opportunities for play (the clinician actively needs to observe play behaviours). Waiting durations from referral to assessment vary across territories, but can typically be extensive. Anyone who suspects that their child is autistic should ideally collate as much 'evidence' as they can to support the assessing clinician's work (as the assessment is after all a small window on the child's life); from general observations and notes from teachers and therapists, to audio or video files of behaviours, and also diaries, kept by the parents. (These diaries can detail behaviours and anxiety levels, and other factors like diet, sleep, events, socialisation, environmental factors, etc).

The autist's view

Assessment and diagnosis are important milestones for autists. It's hard to generalise about what to expect during an adult autism assessment, as each geographical territory and health authority presumably has different procedures; however, I can explain my procedure here in the UK when I was diagnosed in my 40s in 2017, following an increase in my own knowledge-base about autism. (See also the chapter: 'G is for getting used to your autism diagnosis').

Following the discovery of a familial link to autism, I started to recognise that I was probably on the spectrum myself. My GP referred me after an initial consultation (possibly the fact I created a spreadsheet of colour-coded Aspergic traits to show her gave my autisticness away?). It took about six months for the appointment in my region of the UK to come through, which is reportedly very quick.

NHS assessments in my region (at the time of my assessment) were carried out by an independent organisation describing themselves as a 'neurodevelopmental assessment and support service', contracted by the local authority to supply autism assessments for anyone in the region over the age of eight years old. The environment was very relaxed and laid-back, and the office was staffed by very casual and friendly looking people. I arrived and initially saw an assistant clinical psychologist, followed by the consultant counselling psychologist himself, and the whole process took about three hours.

I went in fairly nonchalant, cool, calm and collected; at least that is how I perceived it. When the autism report came back however, it appeared that I was in fact very anxious-looking, displaying several autistic signs, e.g. mis-matching hand-and-vocalisation gestures, and not giving sufficient spontaneous speech. (However, he did note my good eye contact, stating: 'Throughout the assessment, she did use eye contact in a way to initiate, terminate or regulate social interaction, and her eye contact was reasonably well-modulated.' (It is frustrating when individuals and clinicians use the myth that 'autistic people don't make eye contact' as a way of ascertaining a person is not autistic, e.g. if the autistic person is able to make some eye contact. I have seen a paediatrician make this un-true observation. In my opinion, our ability as autists to hold eye contact is (a) learned, and (b) depends on how we're feeling overall; e.g. we may reduce eye-contact depending on how overwhelmed we are). See also the chapter: '*E is for eye contact*'.

The clinician discussed my history and development, family, relationships, education etc and used both the autism diagnostic observations schedule 2nd edition (ADOS-2), and the diagnostic interview of social and communication disorders (DISCO) for the assessment. He was calm and kind and informal throughout, and very patient when I became (unexpectedly) emotional at times.

I left the office with a verbal diagnosis (the written report arrived the following month) feeling a mixture of elation and relief and a jumble of other things; I left the office profusely thanking the psychologist. He may as well have handed me an envelope with big red writing, saying: 'Autism – your new special interest', as that's how it has been for me; literally every day since I started learning about autism and the familial links in our family, I devour information and studies and articles, in an effort to become more well-informed. My diagnosis itself in the written report is autism spectrum disorder, however the clinician verbally described autism with an Asperger's-type profile – although as discussed in the chapters: *A is for Asperger Syndrome*' and '*L is for labels and language*', the term 'Asperger's' is now used less frequently.

I often get asked how friends and family react when someone divulges their autism diagnosis. I'm not sure how it is for every-one, but my initial belief that I may be autistic and my eventual diagnosis was widely met with what I deem to be a kind of am-bivalence by those around me. Someone will of course ask you how it feels to be given an autism diagnosis, and you say things like: 'Well it's a relief really, it's good to be told what I already knew; I always felt different, and now I know why,' etc.

My first few weeks post-autism-diagnosis were spent getting used to the new 'label', telling certain people when the time was right, and having a million lightbulb moments of realisation about my past, my present and my future. As time goes on, as a newly diagnosed autistic, you may well start to question who the real you is; if you're autistic and you made it to adulthood without you or your friends or family knowing about your neurology, you have undoubtedly been masking your struggles, in particular within the social sphere; this may lead you to then question who is the real you. If you're within the workforce, your workmates probably know that you're quirky, but do you have to put on a (probably unconscious) mask to carry out your job? Do you continually seek acceptance, being the natural people pleaser that you are; and in order to nail this social communication thing, do you sometimes use alcohol to help shape your social personality? And if you're a lively social butterfly, is your social personality or persona the real you, or is there a more quiet and passive person underneath? There are many questions.

My clinical psychologist told me that some people don't want to accept their adult autism diagnosis, but that most people are relieved and positive. It is worth remembering that some of the more high-profile autistic people (e.g. broadcaster Chris Packham and actor Anthony Hopkins) did not shout their diagnosis from the rooftops initially, and presumably spent time coming to terms with it and 'finding themselves' before sharing their autistic-selves with other people; this is probably a fine idea, and either way, the autism community is grateful for their honesty.

E is for echolalia

Echolalia, a beautiful-sounding word from the combined Greek words for 'echo' and 'speech', is the repetition of another person's spoken words. It's a valuable part of processing speech for everyone, but for many young autistic individuals, echolalia becomes more than that – part of their persona, and in many cases, part of the 'mask' that helps them fit in with others, including with neurotypical (NT) people. So, echolalia can be considered an early sign of autism.

A simple example of echolalia is if the child replies *'Are you hungry?'*, when asked *'Are you hungry?'* by their parent or carer. (Or perhaps they just repeat the last word – 'hungry'). *"But all children repeat words and phrases – mimicry is just experimenting with different sounds to hone social language skills. It is a normal stage of language development,"* explain incredulous friends and family members to the concerned parent whose child exhibits a lot of echolalia.

Yes. But as with piecing together all autistic signs, it is about spotting patterns and frequencies; looking at the other elements of the child's vocabulary; noticing how their peers talk in the same situation; and noticing whether echolalia is being used to help the child process language. Experts indicate that echolalia, as part of typical language development, has generally *decreased* drastically by the age of three, for typically developing children. Clinicians specialising in autism describe both immediate echolalia and delayed echolalia; immediate echolalia could include our earlier example, e.g. if the child replies *'Are you hungry?'* when asked that same question. It is sometimes an issue of processing (autism is after all primarily said to be a processing difference). The child may be 'buying time', while they're processing the words and their meaning. (Remember, if they're autistic, that there are many things to process in that moment, and 'blocking out' the rest of their environment – e.g. the noisy running tap, the bright bathroom light, the music in the background – may require a few beats of conversation longer. Repeating a question gives them a little more processing time).

Delayed echolalia as an example can take the form of a catch-phrase, song lyric or a line from a TV show. Many people of all neurologies do this of course, but the 'social norm' is to make the phrase relevant to the conversation or situation, and not state it repeatedly. If the child is using a phrase like this, they may have seen the TV show, and they could simply be remembering the episode; but sometimes it is a phrase someone else has vocalised, and makes no real sense comprehensively; it just sounds good!

It can also be a phrase the child has actually heard in real life, often linked to a strong emotion. Maybe they were told off by a teacher, or their parent shouted something in frustration; or maybe the phrase is from a pleasant birthday party, or a foreign holiday (e.g. it can even be a foreign phrase, when the child doesn't speak the language).

"All children repeat words and phrases," reminds the helpful friend or family member, as the five year old jumps off the sofa quoting a phrase from a super-hero film. Yes, but in what situation, and what's the frequency; are they 'stuck' on the phrase like a broken record? Is it said once, five times, ten times maybe? And is it when they're pretending to be the character, or

at tea time? Detective skills are required here, to spot the patterns and frequencies. Also, it's useful to work out what benefit the echolalia has to the child – just a nice, fun sound or phrase that is comforting, or makes them happy? Or a tool to compensate for a lack of language skills?

If it is the first example, bear in mind that autists like 'sameness', and things they know; many will watch a favourite film multiple times, and enjoy the predictability. Maybe a phrase is just part of their appreciation for something predictable in a film. (Also, autists are notorious wordsmiths – just look at some of the most revered, quirky and creative songwriters out there, and ponder whether they have / had autistic traits!) And, if the echolalia is a fun sound or phrase that is comforting, is the comfort needed for good reasons, e.g. as we'd hug a teddy because it feels nice? Or, of more concern, because the child is stressed or anxious? If it's the latter, how can the 'stressors' be lessened? Also, if it's the second scenario, and the child is over the age of three, could speech and language therapy be a consideration?

Autistic individuals may develop a set of social skills or a 'mask' that helps them fit in with others. (See the chapter: 'M is for masking'). Going back to something we mentioned previously in this chapter, echolalia may form part of a 'mask' that helps the autistic child fit in with others, including with NT peers. This element can make it hard for some outsiders to see an issue with a child who may be autistic, but doesn't have a diagnosis. "To infinity and beyond!" shouts the autistic child repeatedly to his or her playmates, as they play space rockets and space-men. It may look as if they are interacting with their peers, that they're all enjoying the game collaboratively, and that the words are used in context – but are they? How are the other children conversing – what vocabulary are they using? And is the child using echolalia as a mask or 'fitting-in' strategy, because he or she is struggling with conventional or typical communication styles? An undiagnosed autistic child has many cues and signs that he or she presents; but noticing them takes the aforementioned detective work, sometimes. The websites: *www.autism-help.org* and *www.speechandlanguagekids.com* have some really useful tips, articles and factsheets on echolalia.

The autist's view

I have very limited experience of echolalia. As a child, I did have a bedtime phrase that was often told to me, but that I managed to get 'stuck' in my head on a loop, whenever I tried to sleep. I added another phrase to it and it became an unwelcome voice, like a stuck record, being played over and over. However as I didn't vocalise it, I don't consider that to be echolalia. It was just part of the 'repetition and rigidity' aspect of autism.

We have an autistic child in our family who has seemingly used echolalia. The child once heard a phrase on the radio, an audio clip from TV's 1970s police drama, 'The Sweeney'. The character DI Jack Regan said: 'Get your trousers on, you're nicked,' and for a time, the child often quoted that phrase at unexpected moments. I expect it was echolalia, but the child loves interesting words, and this is a very comical phrase; and it usually elicited sniggers from grown-ups, which made it even more fun for the child to say. To me, echolalia seems to be something rewarding to the person saying it, and a positive sign for future language skills, in children. However a speech and language therapist could be consulted if families have concerns about their child's use of echolalia.

E is for eye contact

Eye contact is often one of the first things that is referenced with regard to whether someone is autistic, even by supposed experts and autism clinicians. You will sometimes hear some (ill-informed) people say: *"So and so doesn't look very autistic, because they do make eye contact..."* Eye contact is used the world over as a way to initiate, terminate or regulate social interaction. It is absolutely true to say that people on the autistic spectrum struggle at varying degrees to make eye contact. (Very often, they will also have problems being videoed or photographed).

But here are two important points:

- Autistic people can make eye contact. If they do, don't assume they're not autistic!
- However, on such occasions, the autistic person may just be tolerating the eye contact.

Observe the autistic person in question, and there is every chance that if they are making eye contact, then it is just when they are comfortable with it at the minimum level required. It likely goes hand in hand with their current anxiety levels, and even the relationship with the other person. What is uncomfortable for someone on the autistic spectrum is enforced eye contact, and if that situation happens to be at a stressful time, for example a job interview or a one-to-one with a teacher, when the autistic child or adult might feel judged, then their stress responses will be coming into play already. As stress levels increase (or other negative emotions connected with the person they're supposed to be looking at!), the ability of the autistic person to comfortably hold eye contact reduces. *"Look at me when I am speaking to you!"* shouted by a cross parent to an autistic child will likely be crushing for the autist. At stressful times, making eye contact is harder for most autists. We can simplify the issue by saying that in non-stressful situations, many autistic people are able to hold eye contact, but it doesn't mean that they are very accomplished at it, or very comfortable with it; just that they have learned that it's expected, and that they can certainly do it when there is a real need to! However, it may be a kind of mask, e.g. the autistic person is acting in a neurotypical (NT) way, because they know it is expected.

However, if shutdown is imminent (see the chapter: *'S is for shutdown'*), e.g. if an autistic person is feeling stressed or threatened, or if there is any underlying issue with the person that they're supposed to be making eye contact with (e.g. a conflict or argument or an area of mistrust), then the autistic person will find it difficult to look them in the eye. Also, you can sometimes look more closely at the autistic person's eye gaze, and a lot of the time, you may find that they are not making direct contact with the other person's eyes, but perhaps just below the eyes, for example 'nose' contact, or above the eyes, e.g. 'eyebrow' contact! (Which is a great compromise for all concerned, in this author's opinion). Essentially, extended eye contact is part of a set of learned skill-sets that the autistic person feels they need (or is told they need), in order to appear typical.

So, a plea to families and friends of autists – please don't focus on eye contact being a definitive assessment of whether a person is autistic or not – autistic people can and do make eye contact, but it is invariably hard for them, and their ability to do so could be an indicator of their discomfort or stress levels. (This author is certainly against any 'compliance'-based training or so-called therapy that enforces eye contact for an autistic person). Interestingly, a feature on the website Scientist Alert sourcing a study from the journal 'Nature Scientific Reports' states that: *'Researchers have discovered a part of the brain responsible for helping new-borns turn towards familiar faces is abnormally activated among those on the autism spectrum, suggesting therapies that force eye contact could inadvertently be inducing anxiety.'* (Source: *www.tiny.cc/eye-contact*).

Researchers concluded that avoiding eye contact as an autistic person: *"Is a way to decrease an unpleasant excessive arousal, stemming from over-activation in a particular part of the brain."* [The subcortical system]. It is also of value to think about why the eye contact is taking place, e.g. why an autistic person would tolerate something that's uncomfortable for them – NT people use eye contact to share 'socio-emotional' messages. However, even when the autistic person is making eye contact, it is probably more for function, and to gain information (or meet an expectation), rather than to share an emotional 'moment'. In an autism assessment, the assessor will take the patient's eye contact into account, but (if they're experienced as a clinician), will take it into account as a broader part of the overall picture, and will also note how the person being assessed uses their non-verbal gestures as well.

The autist's view

As mentioned in the chapter: *'D is for diagnosis'*, my diagnosing clinician noted my good eye contact, stating: 'Throughout the [autism] assessment, she did use eye contact in a way to initiate, terminate or regulate social interaction, and her eye contact was reasonably well-modulated.' Frustratingly, a different health care professional, a child's paediatrician, once implied that I didn't 'look autistic', as I made eye contact. I believe that our ability as autists to hold eye contact is (a) learned, and (b) depends on how we're feeling overall. I don't believe eye contact should be enforced. Remember that study researchers have found that avoiding eye contact as an autistic person decreases 'unpleasant excessive arousal', which makes sense when some autists describe eye contact as being painful.

F is for
films and media

This chapter looks at some of the representations of autism in the media. Until fairly recently, there was relatively little content on autism in the broadcast media; but the last five years (at the time of writing) has seen that situation change massively. (There's a great article on the Public Broadcasting Service's website about autism on the screen, at: *www.tiny.cc/autism_films*).

Rainman (Let's get this one out of the way first)

In recent memory of course, the most obvious media representation of autism is probably the film *Rainman*, a movie best described as 'of its time', depicting the journey of an autistic savant played by neurotypical (NT) actor, Dustin Hoffman. Rainman has its detractors of course, and there are many issues of contention with it. The website Interacting With Autism writes about some of the issues in their article on media representations of autism, quoting an expert as saying – *'There is a danger of walking away from the movie with the impression that all autistic persons are savants, and that all savants are autistic; the film concludes that [Raymond], and presumably other individuals with autism, are better off being institutionalised rather than living with their own family.'* (Source: *www.tiny.cc/autism_films2*).

But many autists recognise the film's important contribution, and nuanced elements. Cassie and Therese at the website

Autism Myth Busters write: '*As Charlie learns to truly love his brother as the movie unfolds, Raymond too seems to have 'opened up' and created a lasting emotional attachment with his newly reunited brother... [while] Raymond's development of a loving bond with his brother should not be seen as him 'overcoming' his autism, it should be viewed as a relationship developed because of his autism.*' (Source: *www.tiny.cc/autism_films3*).

The Good Doctor

Elsewhere, Freddie Highmore's recent 'autistic savant' part in TV's The Good Doctor, while drawing praise for its inclusion of a main autistic character (although Highmore is not autistic), drew criticism from some quarters for yet another 'savant' character with a Hollywood Disability Superpower. (In fact, savantism of these kinds is rare). However, many autists welcomed Highmore's performance, and the show as a whole. Writing on the website *www.slate.com*, autist Sara Luterman states approvingly: '*Freddie Highmore is not autistic, although he does a decent job portraying one of us on TV. When he plays Dr. Shaun Murphy, he has an 'autism accent', that unusual cadence that many of us speak with. He holds his body the way I hold my body. It's the best representation of an autistic person I've ever seen on television.*' (Source: *www.tiny.cc/autism_films4*).

Atypical

In Netflix's *Atypical*, the autistic main character, Sam, is described by Sara Luterman for *www.slate.com* more disapprovingly as 'hollow inside'. '*Autistic people rarely get portrayed as real, complete human beings. In Atypical, [he's] essentially a diagnostic checklist, not a whole person. He's hollow inside – there's nothing in his mind except sex and penguins. The show isn't really about Sam. The show is about Sam's autism, and how it affects Sam's family. He is, in many ways, a plot device in what is supposed to be his own story.'*

The Curious Incident Of The Dog In The Night-time

The Curious Incident Of The Dog In The Night-time is a book (and subsequent play) that, despite drawing praise for having a main character who has Asperger's Syndrome, is actually a fairly uncomfortable read. The depictions are said by many to be somewhat inaccurate, and actually could be seen to be damaging to autists, promoting the view that autists have no empathy, may be aggressive, and are easily abused by others. At least, that's how many autists feel! Now, the publishers of the book don't even describe the main character as being autistic or having Asperger's, presumably due to the criticism. The author told the Hay Festival audience in 2012 that he had never specified any disorder [when writing the book], and was uncomfortable with the book's status as 'A handbook for autistic spectrum disorders'. The author told the UK's Telegraph newspaper in 2019: *'I'm a little worried if people are saying: if you want to work out how to treat people on the spectrum, read this novel.'*

Other programmes featuring autism

There are a number of further programmes featuring autism – here are some recent examples of autism representation on TV:

Broadcaster Chris Packham's fantastic, ground-breaking UK TV documentary, 'Asperger's and Me'.

Autistic actress Talia Grant being cast in UK TV's Hollyoaks.

Autistic actor Jules Robertson's role in UK TV's *Holby City*.

UK TV's *The A-word* – with autistic cast-member (Travis Smith), and a lead character (Joe Hughes), who's autistic.

The character Saga Noren from the acclaimed Scandinavian TV crime drama, *The Bridge* – Noren is widely said to be autistic.

Julia, the USA's *Sesame Street* autistic muppet/puppet. (Although TV producers have since drawn massive criticism after they used the character for American Public Service Announcements produced with an autism organisation that many autists do not support, endorse or engage with. The campaign has been criticised as stigmatising autistic children and their families).

The UK's CBeebies' animation, *Pablo*, with an autistic cast.

The USA's *Power Rangers'* Billy Blue Ranger (played by RJ Cyler) – a fictional autistic super-hero.

The UK's Channel 4's '*Are You Autistic?*' – an 'intro-level' programme with some interesting elements, presented by autists.

Finally, as a side-note, this author also enjoyed an online article called 'Autism is a creative boon – a list and celebration of 5 openly autistic actors, musicians, and artists', by E Price, who writes about the 'usual' autistic 'celebs', but in more detail than is usually seen. (See: *www.tiny.cc/autism_media*).

The autist's view

It is positive to see more autistic characters depicted on screen with storylines that aren't necessarily about their autism. Raymond in *Rainman* is obviously the 'go to' autistic character, but I don't see it as a misrepresentation of autism exactly; more a (somewhat dated) amplification of a character trope. UK TV's *The A-word* is a programme that my family and I really enjoyed; it is well-written, funny and touching.

G is for getting used to your autism diagnosis

This author goes into more detail of the experience of an adult autism assessment at the end of the chapter: *'D is for diagnosis'*, in 'The autist's view'. But here's some further insight into what happens after an autism assessment, taken from the popular *www.spectra.blog* entry: *'So, you have had your adult autism assessment – what now?'*. It was written to support newly diagnosed autists themselves, and the content uses the word 'you', to address the autist.

You may feel liberated, relieved, excited, thankful, validated, and may experience any number of positive emotions; it seems that on the whole, most people gaining autism diagnosis in adulthood find it a positive experience. But, like any life-changing event, a range of emotions will probably come into play at some point; an interesting one is anger; perhaps with family members, or The System – so be prepared for some emotions that you didn't expect.

Undoubtedly, there will be some extended family members and friends that you may be wondering how to explain your autism diagnosis to. It is pertinent that some older friends and family members will not have had the same exposure to the information that is available nowadays, and their experiences of autism will be very different, and possibly negative. You may wonder how to describe yourself. Autistic person? Person with autism? Autist? (You can read more in the chapter: *'L is for la-*

bels and language'). You might find it difficult trying to explain your autism diagnosis to other people, and it's quite likely that along your imminent journey, people will say things to you that aren't deemed to be insightful or helpful: For example: *'But you don't look autistic!' 'Well, it must be very mild.' 'Don't worry, it doesn't change you as a person.'* (It does). *'But you look us in the eye, how can you be autistic?'*

Some people that you tell may draw to mind some friend or family member that they believe to be on the autistic spectrum, and will regale you with 'positive' stories about their bravery against adversity, and how the individual sometimes, almost occasionally, now and then at least, appears to be something close to 'normal'! Many people, and these may be the ones that know you the best, will be completely supportive but reasonably ambivalent, as if you had told them that you'd taken up a new hobby or found a new favourite food. In any case, when to tell people about your autism is very much down to you, now you're going about your everyday life with a new autism diagnosis.

This autism diagnosis is probably one of the single most significant things that has happened to you to date; and yes, people including yourself go through illness, parenthood, romance, tragedy and all manner of Big Life Experiences; and surely an autism diagnosis is small fry, compared to these big life milestones?

Well actually, an autism spectrum disorder diagnosis for an adult is potentially 'bigger' than just about everything else, for the simple reason that it is the frame or filter from which you look at all of these experiences and milestones; it is your window on the world – the thing that defines how you react to everything around you – and almost everyone will underestimate how big this milestone (an autism diagnosis) is for you. Many people close to you will undoubtedly feel happy that you have your diagnosis, as it gives you some kind of closure, validation, clarity or affirmation; but it is unlikely that they will realise how life changing it will be for you; and that is okay. It's your journey. You may not have anticipated that for many newly-diagnosed autists, the diagnosis gives them a new perspective on the people around them, e.g. their workmates, friends and family members – and there is a good chance that this new perspective allows you (as the autist) to see more clearly just how people feel about you.

If you are used to masking (putting on a more neurotypical 'face' or persona to get you through life's daily social situations – see the chapter: 'M is for masking'), you may find that you are less comfortable with this masking after your diagnosis; this is because you probably weren't doing it consciously for a lot of the time. And if you are now more comfortable in yourself, and with showing the 'real you', you may notice that some of the people in your 'life circle' do not have your best interests at heart; and this may result in some social or familial 'culling', as you become more perceptive of the people around you, and their intentions. (Talking therapies can help with the process of working out who you find supportive, and benefit from having in your life). At the same time, you may possibly notice with a renewed clarity the people that matter the most to you; the ones that respect you, like you for who you are, understand your quirks, and are interested in your life and are respectful of you; and these are the people that surely count.

An important and fun element of your new autism diagnosis is the 'autie-dar' that comes with it, as you will have been researching autism ahead of your diagnosis, and your knowledge-base is probably pretty impressive. You will undoubtedly (due to the prevalence of a genetic autism link) have noticed that some people in your family (close or extended) also have autistic traits;

you will apply this new 'superpower' to those around you, and may start noticing people in the media and in the spotlight, as well as people at work, children at your own children's school, as well as friends and extended family members, who could be autistic. Whether or not you want to point this out to any of them is a different matter!

Telling your work colleagues or even stating your autism status on a job application is a very tricky subject, and one that is always going to come down to individual circumstances. There is hopefully a good possibility that if you are employed, telling your work superiors about the fact you're autistic could work in your favour, in terms of organising some strategies that would help you be more productive at work. For example, arranging a more private workstation, less involvement in open table meetings and brainstorming sessions, negotiating a reduction in the sociable aspects of the job, making a reduction in sensory overload (in terms of lights and noises and sensory stimulation) – or whatever elements would work, in your own professional circumstances. In terms of declaring your autism on a job application, that is a very personal matter, and you should probably take advice based around your individual circumstances.

One of the big questions is; where do I go now? In terms of, how can I use the new diagnostic information to help make the rest of my life better? If you have only just received a diagnosis of autism and you are an adult, you have undoubtedly faced some instability in life, both physically and mentally – this will have impacted your life, and there are many mental health issues associated with autism that are exacerbated by a lack of self-care (which for example can include taking time to de-stress and recover from 'social hangovers' or over-socialisation, and having some non-social time to enjoy your own interests, and catch up on sleep and down-time). So now it's time as a newly diagnosed autist to work out your self-care plan, moving forward, and perhaps establish more contentment. E.g. maybe you need to cut down on things that use up your emotional bandwidth and energy – for example, excessive social engagements that you never really enjoyed anyway; mingling with people that don't enhance your life, within your social scene (perhaps linked to the workplace or your partner, e.g. not of your choosing); or any situation that is not really benefiting you!

Let's say it again – it is perhaps time to try to cut down on things that use up your emotional bandwidth; especially if you're working too many hours and if you have too many family responsibilities and life challenges, generally. In light of your autism diagnosis, if something's not suiting you and benefiting you, now is a great time to make some changes; this is after all the first day of the rest of your life – and you deserve to live in an optimal way, getting the very best out of it!

The autist's view

I would say to newly diagnosed autists that hopefully your autism diagnosis has allowed you to find out more about yourself, understand what makes you tick, and realise that you're not a failing neurotypical, but an outstanding autist (or whichever self-identity you prefer, or fits!) You have every right to thrive in whatever situation you choose. So, if life was holding you back, now is the time to leave the past's challenges where they belong (in the past), forge your own way, and let your autistic star shine.

H is for hangover (social)

One of hardest issues to deal with when autistic can be the 'social hangover' – the after-effects of socialisation that deplete an autist's energy. Let's explore this concept further. Firstly, it's important to realise that all autists use many, many 'spoons' or energy units when they socialise; and that includes socialisation with their family. Not heard of the spoons theory? It was developed quite by chance by Christine Miserandino, who has lupus, and uses 'spoons' to explain how to ration one's energy. (The information here is partly replicated in the chapter: *'S is for spoons theory'.)* The spoons theory, a kind of disability metaphor, states that a person with a reduction in energy levels (emotional or physical), starts the day with a certain number of spoons. Each spoon represents a burst of energy; so showering, getting dressed etc requires small numbers of spoons, as does conversing with close friends and family at home. Some activities, for example, meeting a group of friends or colleagues, being interviewed, chatting in a public place, require lots of spoons. Therefore, autists often find that, due to their autistic challenges – e.g. social communication and social interaction issues, as well as sensory challenges – great chunks of their energy may be used up more quickly than that of their neurotypical (NT) peers and family members. And what happens when an autist socialises – even with friends or family that they love and enjoy spending time with? They use up lots of spoons!

Let's take an average day for a busy working autist Mum; let's say she has 12 spoons of (mainly emotional) energy that day, which was Christine Miserandino's original proposition.

Get up and complete the morning duties and the school run. Two spoons.

Do a few hours at her part time job. Four spoons.

Do the school run and complete the afternoon family duties. Two spoons.

Cook tea and manage the child's bedtime regime. Two spoons.

Converse with her family. Two spoons.

That's all her energy used up.

But what if something unexpected happens – e.g. a phone call from a relative that was emotionally draining; a long chat at the school gates with a fellow parent; an impromptu talk with the teacher; or a neighbour wanting to chat? These require spoons, and our theoretical autist Mum has none left. In an ideal world, she would realise her spoon allocation had 'run over' that day, and would plan for a quieter day the next day, to recalibrate. Maybe using self-care tools like headphone-time listening to music, reading a book, having a nap, or whatever works for her.

But what if our Mum wanted to arrange some social time with a friend or family? Dinner perhaps, a little shopping spree, time at the park with the kids, a trip to a local attraction? It's likely this would use up a massive part of her daily spoon allowance. (Especially as there's very likely to be background music, extra lighting, or noisy chatter thrown into the sensory melting pot). So, she'd have to plan for both a low-spoon day on the day of the social visit, and probably the next day too, to recalibrate. If her spoon-management wasn't up to speed, our autist would likely suffer from a 'social hangover', whereby she'd need downtime from most conversation and interaction, and probably sensory stimulation, until she recovered. (Otherwise autistic shutdown may ensue – see the chapter: 'S is for shutdown'). So, it is important for friends and family members of autists (children and adults alike) to realise that, no matter how much the autist may want to see you or converse with you, their energy bank (or emotional cutlery drawer!) is finite. Days out, family parties, Christmas events, visiting relatives and the like can be exhausting for autists. It's important as an autist to plan one's social calendar carefully in relation to the rest of the week, to limit social hangovers. And imagine what a social hangover is like for an autistic child, who maybe can't grasp their emotional cutlery drawer needs, or explain or understand why they're mentally exhausted? Family members of autistic children ideally need to factor in enough down time, so the child doesn't get too run down or spoon-deficient. Please also see the chapter: 'K is for Knowing your own spectrum', which details how autists may also be in a 'spectrum within a spectrum', e.g. with slow days, fast days and recovery days.

The autist's view

Finding out about the spoons theory and the issue of social hangovers was immensely useful to me. The aspect that many NT individuals don't understand is that the autist may want to spend time with them – the third party – but their emotional bandwidth capacity is full, or used up. It is respectful of friends and family members to recognise that the autist needs downtime away from communication and socialisation. This is especially true at times that are conventionally very busy, like religious holidays and birthdays. Autistic children especially should be given sufficient 'recovery time' to get over their social hangover.

I is for influencers

This chapter looks at high-profile individuals forging a positive path, and raising awareness of autism. Whilst there are many fantastic #actuallyautistic autism advocates blogging, vlogging and writing about autism, this chapter *isn't* about them – rather, it's about individuals who are well-known for something else.

Influencers are individuals with an influence in a sector – so for this author, an influencer in the autism sector is someone who (a) is autistic, (b) is a positive role model, (c) speaks positively about autism, and (d) has a public profile. Here, this author would like to highlight some specific individuals. Before ploughing on however, it's important to acknowledge that there are handfuls of fabulously talented and well-respected individuals who are autistic, and have a high-profile. (Some are referenced in the online article: *'Autism is a creative boon – a list and celebration of 5 openly autistic actors, musicians, and artists'*, by E Price, at: *www.tiny.cc/autism_media*).

These individuals include:

Actress Daryl Hannah: "[Growing up] I didn't fit in anywhere... Anything that involves meeting or talking to more than a couple of people scares the hell out of me," she told Australia's Women's Weekly magazine.

Musician Gary Newman: "[My Asperger's] has given me a slightly different view of the world and I truly believe it helped get me through some hard times. I'd never wish it away," he told the Irish News.

Actor Sir Anthony Hopkins: "[Yes], I realised early that [my] brain just worked in a way that was more conducive to acting and art than perhaps business. [But] I didn't know Asperger's even existed." (Source: Lidz, Fessier and Gannon, reported on *www.psychologymatters.asia*).

Road-racer and broadcaster Guy Martin: "[My Asperger's] is probably what helps me with endurance racing on my mountain bike. I'm not quick but I'm good at getting my head down," he told the Sunday Times.

British Para-gold-medallist swimmer Jessica-Jane Applegate MBE: "My classification is S14- a swimmer with an intellectual impairment. I really struggle with pacing sets, clocks, reading, writing, remembering how to do things, multi-tasking and communication. I was diagnosed with Asperger's as a teenager – but this if anything has helped me, because I practice and practice until I get it right," she told 'Autism and Sport'. (Source: *www.tiny.cc/jessicaA*).

And footballer Lionel Messi, who is widely acknow-ledged to be autistic: "When he enters the area, he knows he will score. And he celebrates, with that typical autistic smile, one who has fulfilled his mission and is relieved," – the views of Roberto Amado, journalist. (Source: *www.tiny.cc/messi*).

But for this author, to be an autism influencer, it isn't enough just to have a public profile and to be autistic, as is the case for the above individuals. Yes, there are high profile autists out there, all fabulously accomplished and respected people; but these indi-viduals rarely give interviews specifically about being autists, or promote their 'autisticness'; and why on earth should they? Autism doesn't define them! Many autists excel as artistic performers and athletes – perhaps their autism, with its links to attention to detail and preference for repetition and perfectionism, helps them achieve the highest echelons within their field?

(Incidentally, a reportedly high number of technology business leaders and members of the 'tech' workforce are autistic. The computer science company SAP forecasts that by 2020, 1% of its 65,000 employees will be autistic. The engineering start up Ultranauts has an impressive 75% of autists in its workforce. Interestingly, the fantastic book Neurotribes started as an investigation into the prevalence of autism within the 'tech bubble' workplace of America's Silicon Valley. (See: *www.tiny.cc/Neurotribes)*. Perhaps autism's links to problem solving, not getting caught up in emotional distractions and logical decision-making are factors in some autists' success in their careers?)

So; as mentioned, the 'famous' autists that we know of, including those listed above, don't regularly give interviews specifically about being autistic. No one in the public eye has to be any kind of ambassador or influencer for their neurology; but we'd like to celebrate some that are.

Chris Packham CBE

British naturalist and broadcaster Chris Packham was diagnosed with Asperger Syndrome in his forties (see the chapter: '*A is for Asperger Syndrome'*) and has undoubtedly made a world of difference to autists, thanks to his ground-breaking UK TV documentary, 'Asperger's And Me': "*Chris experiences the world in a very different way, with heightened senses that at times are overwhelming, and a mind that is constantly bouncing from one subject to the next,"* the UK's BBC reported. From championing the late autist Alan Turing in the BBC's 'Greatest Person of the 20th Century' icons project, to being an ambassador for the National Autistic Society, Chris has done a great deal to help autists come to terms with their autism (in this author's opinion), and describes his own Asperger's as a gift. *"[It was] difficult positioning myself to represent the autistic community; because it's impossible. I am not a typical autistic person – because there isn't a typical autistic person,"* Chris told supporters via his website *www.chrispackham.co.uk*, after his TV programme was shown. *"We [autistic individuals] don't need a cure, there is nothing wrong with us – we are different,"* he added. (Incidentally, Chris has drawn criticisms from some social media participants regarding his views on disability and its relation to autism; however this author's view is that he is surely entitled to his own opinions?)

Anne Hegerty

Anne Hegerty is famous in the UK as a 'quizzer', and plays the Governess on UK TV's 'The Chase'. She also entered the jungle on UK TV's 'I'm a celebrity get me out of here' in 2018, when she won over viewers. Anne told The National Autistic Society: *"[Gaining an autism diagnosis] made me feel better... I feel if people ever say to me 'I understand [that] you identify as autistic', actually I don't do any 'identifying' at all. Objectively, I conform to scientific criteria drawn up by people who aren't me... I kind of feel that distinction is important. What I do mind a bit is people going around claiming that they are neuro-atypical, and I think what they mean is simply they are depressed and anxious, shy and introverted... it's perfectly possible to be a shy introvert, who's not on the spectrum at all."* On UK TV's The Wright Stuff, Anne gave possibly the best ever autism quote, when she said: *"People say you suffer from Asperger's. No, I have Asperger's; I suffer from idiots."*

Talia and Carrie Grant

Talia Grant is a young British actress who got her big break on UK TV's young adult 'soap', Hollyoaks. Along with mum Carrie, Talia is a great ambassador for neurodiversity. Talia was the first female autistic actress to land a mainstream British TV role in her part as autist Brooke Hathaway and has admitted that autism 'can be a gift and a curse'. *"I know that I'm not like everyone else,"* Talia told the BBC. *"My character Brooke has faced those difficulties and challenges of feeling different. I would have loved to have someone growing up that had autism, that was open about it, that was an actor that I could resonate with."* Talia seems to be a very mature young woman, and has taken the pressure of being a role model very well. The show itself is seemingly addressing diversity in earnest, with Hollyoaks featuring a 'diversity special', and reportedly boasting an autistic writer on its writing team. All potentially great news for young autists who are watching the programme, and learning about neurominorities.

Talia's Mum, vocal coach Carrie Grant, has also spoken extensively about neurodiversity, saying on the website: *www.carrieanddavidgrant.co.uk*, which she shares with husband and fellow vocal coach David Grant: *"I am Mum to four children; three birth, one adopted, three with ADHD, two autistic... all high functioning, so they can appear much of the time to be just like everyone else around them."* Often in the media, we see parents of autists speaking about their children's issues in a negative light, maybe in connection with a loss of local support services, or the challenges that living in a family with an autist brings. However, the Grants are, as a family, exceptional ambassadors for autism and neurodiversity. *"We have encouraged our children to be proud of being their autistic selves. A label is only a problem if you have a problem with the label,"* Carrie states.

Ethan Fineshriber

Ethan Fineshriber is an American martial artist who has played the Green Ranger on Ninja Kidz TV, and has achieved a second-degree black belt. He was diagnosed as being autistic as a young child, and rose to fame when he won his first world title with a perfect score in the XMA (Extreme Martial Arts) black belt boys' division of the ATA (American Taekwondo Association). You can see Ethan's vlogs, which include brilliant films about autism, on his You Tube page – (see: *www.tinycc/ethanF*). Ethan's Mother Mara told Autism Parenting' Magazine: *"I am one of the proudest mothers on the planet and I take heart in knowing that while Ethan will still always struggle with some things, and will always be a little quirky in some ways, he sincerely has the world at his feet. He has the willpower and fortitude needed to achieve anything he can dream of."*

Greta Thunberg

The teen Swede and Nobel Peace Prize nominee was thrust into the limelight after initiating a weekly school strike to protest about the lack of Government action to address issues surrounding global climate change. At the time writing, she is arguably one of the most famous people in the world, let alone the most famous autistic person. She's addressed world leaders, spoken at the UN's climate-change conference in Poland, been interviewed on international TV news broadcasts, been featured on magazine covers, and has given inspirational TED Talks. Importantly, Greta doesn't shy away from talking about her

Asperger's diagnosis. What's fascinating is that autism is clearly a driving force behind her passion for tackling climate change. Greta previously suffered from depression and issues with eating, in what could represent autistic burnout. In her TED Talk (see: *www.tinycc/Greta_T*), she explained how, at the age of eleven, several years after learning about the concept of climate change for the first time, she fell into a depression and became ill. "*I stopped talking. I stopped eating. In two months, I lost about ten kilos of weight. Later on I was diagnosed with Asperger's Syndrome, OCD, and selective mutism; that basically means I only speak when I think it's necessary.*" However, Greta turned this personal crisis around to become a respected activist, telling the UK's Independent newspaper that her autism helps her see things from outside the box. "*It makes me different, and being different is a gift, I would say.*" Described as 'The Joan of Arc of climate change' by the title Intelligencer, Greta's typically Asperger's-esque vocal delivery, whilst it has drawn its detractors and unkind 'trolls' online, has always been direct, matter-of-fact, and disarming. In this author's opinion, she is a fantastic role model and worthy influencer.

The autist's view

There may be many more autism influencers, in addition to the many #actuallyautistic autism advocates spreading the word about neurodiversity, that I haven't included here; however the above people are the individuals that have garnered my interest the most recently. We need people who are honest yet positive about their autism talking openly about their diagnosis, so that young people who are in a neurominority have role models to look up to.

J is for
jigsaw puzzle piece

This chapter is quite personal, in that it is the author's opinion – although it is one that's widely held by other autistic individuals. It is still surprising to this author how often one sees the autism puzzle piece. It's a contentious issue – the jigsaw puzzle piece is frequently used as a logo to promote autism products, charities, entities and awareness events.

Conceived in 1963 by Gerald Gasson, a parent and board member for the National Autistic Society (or NAS, formerly The Society for Autistic Children), the puzzle piece was used as the board reportedly believed that autistic people suffered from a 'puzzling' condition. (The NAS no longer uses the graphic). Many individuals nowadays object to the puzzle piece's use in autism awareness campaigns; public opinion is fairly divided, however. Here's this author's view. The people opposing the jigsaw puzzle piece often find it patronising as it implies that autistic individuals are part of a big puzzle that needs to be fixed. It also has strong connotations with an American autism organisation who arguably have done very little for autism acceptance. Further criticisms about the jigsaw puzzle logo are that it is invariably shown in bright primary colours, thus linking it to children, when autism is in fact a neurology concerning people of all ages. Furthermore, bright, primary colours are hardly conducive to people with sensory challenges!

On the other hand, there are many people who really don't have an opinion about the puzzle piece one way or another, or even quite like its depiction of a puzzle. In their defence, some people would argue that autism is indeed puzzling, and that the puzzle pieces simply represent the concept of fitting together, or fitting in. Although (judging by discussions on social media, at least), opinion does seem fairly evenly split (perhaps down to a lack of education as to why objectors are offended by the jigsaw puzzle piece logo!), to generalise, it seems that most objectors to the puzzle piece are autistic adults, while those less offended are parents of autistic children, or those working in the field of autism who aren't autistic themselves. But in this enlightened time, it does seem sensible to move onto a more widely accepted logo with less historically negative links; for example the infinity logo on the cover of this book, which represents diversity, and is seemingly much more widely preferred. Recently, some autism organisations have changed their marketing materials as a direct result of autistic individuals enlightening them as to why the puzzle pieces used may cause offence; a very positive step!

Also, don't take this author's word for it – a study titled: '*Do puzzle pieces and autism puzzle piece logos evoke negative associations?*', which researched public perception and was published in the journal 'Autism', stated: '*If an autism organization's intention for using puzzle-piece imagery is to evoke negative associations, then the use of puzzle-piece imagery is apt. If, instead, an autism organization's intention for using puzzle-piece imagery is not meant to devalue autistic persons, but, quite the opposite, to celebrate [autistic persons], our results suggest that puzzle-piece imagery should probably be avoided.*' (Source: *www.tiny.cc/jigsawpuzzle*).

Along the same lines as this author's observations about the jigsaw puzzle piece, it is worth noting within this chapter that many autistic individuals are not fans of the 'Light it up blue' campaigns that arise each spring, around the time of autism awareness month. Various buildings, normally backlit with plain lights, have blue filters added at the time of the campaign, as some kind of 'tribute to', or 'to promote awareness of' autism. The origins of the concept lie with the same aforementioned American organisation that has arguably done little to promote autism acceptance. The majority of autistic individuals (seemingly especially in the UK), who know of the 'Light it up blue' origins, do not support the campaign, with many successfully asking project organisers who adopt the 'Light it up blue' concept to change the filter colours used, to support the neurodiversity movement.

In conclusion within this chapter, what #actuallyautistic advocates and many families of autists crave is acceptance. Surely, all that the 'awareness' elements like dated puzzle piece logos and campaigns like 'Light it up blue' do is enhance awareness that autism exists? They don't generally educate anyone about autism, and acceptance of neurodiversity and neurominorities. They're sometimes accompanied with stories of parents 'bravely revealing' their child is autistic, or tales of an individual 'suffering with autism'; e.g. unhelpful language that does nothing for true awareness of the fact that autism is widely considered to be a lifelong processing difference.

The autist's view

It is pleasing that many organisations are 'dropping' the dated puzzle piece. But this issue forms part of a larger debate about awareness and education. I believe that the way we are exposed to autism isn't helped by the lack of really positive influencers in the media, and on social media. We will all come into contact with hundreds of autists in our lifetime; autistic individuals are represented by our families, our children's teachers, our work colleagues, etc. Everyday autistic people getting on with their lives! However, in the media, references to autism are more commonly the aforementioned 'celebs' who 'bravely' discuss their autistic family member. (Not that I believe that this exposure and ambassadorship is intrinsically a bad thing; of course it isn't – however, it is the negative language used, usually by presenters or journalists, that sometimes irks).

Of course, there are some excellent advocates and autism influencers around – there are very many #actuallyautistic bloggers, and also a select number of high-profile media people whose work to raise acceptance is appreciated; see the chapter: 'I is for influencers'. However, more well-informed presenters and journalists, more #actuallyautistic advocates in the spotlight, (especially on TV), and more education all-round, in terms of acceptable 'awareness' campaigns and marketing assets, would definitely be a step forward for the autism community! I think I have covered 'the autist's view' of the autism puzzle piece, as this chapter is my personal opinion, and not necessarily reflective of what everyone within the autism community thinks. Hopefully it offers some insight into why many individuals are not fans of the jigsaw graphic, however!

J is for judgements

This chapter on judgement aims to help inform friends and family members of individuals who believe their child may be autistic, as well as educators who have been approached by parents with the same concerns.

The chapter isn't designed to belittle anyone for their lack of knowledge about autism. For example, outside of psychiatry circles, no-one had much awareness of autism until at least the 1990s; and the element of the UK Government's teacher training framework that taught educators how to support children with special educational needs, especially autistic children, reportedly wasn't rolled out until 2016. This implies that many teaching or support staff members may still lack some experience in the field. The end result is that, thanks to a wide array of information on autism being available to today's parents, their own family members (especially older relatives), often simply haven't had the exposure to the autism education and awareness that we enjoy today. And teachers and educators who haven't received specific autism training, or haven't taught autistic children in their class, also may not be fully up to date with the latest schools of thought. Hence, this chapter aims to help extended family members and educators understand the most helpful responses, if someone's shared concerns that a child may be autistic.

What not to say...

Here's what isn't helpful as a response, however well-meaning, to a parent who's expressed the view that their child could have autism:

I am sure there's nothing wrong with him.

All children do that!

But she doesn't look autistic.

Normal people do that too.

I wouldn't worry – we're all a little bit autistic, aren't we?

She will grow out of it.

Maybe it's a discipline issue?

You're spending too much time on the internet, looking for conditions that aren't there.

But he can hold eye contact!

She is completely fine at school. Maybe the problem is the home environment?

Maybe he's reacting to your anxiety?

Autism wasn't prevalent in my day.

My friend's son is autistic, and she doesn't act like him at all.

More helpful reactions could be:

Can you share some of your resources with me? I'd like to know more.

What can I do to help, in the way of research or reading?

She may not be autistic – but assuming it's a possibility; what can I do to help reduce her challenges, or make her feel less anxious?

Wow. That's a lot for you to be dealing with as a family. How are you feeling? (Or, how do your concerns make you feel?)

What are the next steps for you, and is there anything I can do to support you?

And for educators:

If the teacher lacks exposure to autistic children, or hasn't had the experience in terms of spotting the very subtle cues of autism that are shown as autistic children develop:

Let's talk to the school SENCO about your concerns.

I will observe the child in the classroom and note down any anxiety-related behaviours, or reactions to social or sensory situations.

I will talk to any colleagues at the school with experience of un-diagnosed autism cases, to see if they have any procedures or experiences that we can draw from.

Autism and education

In terms of educators, Mark Lever, Chief Executive of the National Autistic Society states: "*More than 1 in 100 children are on the autism spectrum. So every teacher will have autistic students in their classes at some point in their careers and they deserve to be given the understanding and skills they need to teach autistic children effectively. Teachers don't need to be experts in autism. A fundamental knowledge of what it means to be autistic and the often simple adjustments that can help, could transform the experience of autistic pupils at school.*"

It's worth noting that if a parent has expressed concerns to a teacher or SENCO about their child, their concerns should be taken seriously, even if absolutely no obvious signs or behaviours are seen at school. (Read more about SEN support in schools at this link: *www.tiny.cc/SENsupport*).

The National Autistic Society states: '*Before your child is identified as needing SEN support in school, the class teacher and SENCO should make an analysis of their needs, using the teacher's assessment and experience and evidence of their progress, attainment and behaviour. Your views and your child's views should also be taken into account. You should always be consulted and kept informed of any action taken to help your child and of the outcome of this.*'

We hope this chapter is useful, or provides food for thought for any parents struggling to get family members or educators to 'believe' their concerns that a child is autistic. Essentially, when responding to a parent's concerns, the author believes it's generally unhelpful to start a sentence with 'I am sure', unless you're clinically qualified to diagnose autism. As this can seem judgemental or belittling to the parent!

The autist's view

It's always a good idea for parents to document their concerns about whether their child is autistic via diaries, videos etc. These assets can be useful to show educators, doctors and health visitors (for pre-school children), and shows that the parent has done their research, and is serious about their concerns. A benefit of keeping a diary is that any behavioural patterns can be spotted, and links made to external factors. Elements like sleep, nutrition, social responses, anxiety and any patterns of behaviours (and their timings, e.g. within an hour of leaving school), can all be noted. To conclude the chapter, this author is not trying to be judgemental about other people's lack of exposure and experience to autism; but simply wants to raise some interesting points of debate that could help parents on their journey towards their child's assessment for autism.

K is for knowing your own autistic spectrum

This chapter is quite personal, as it relates to the author's own experiences; however it has become one of the most popular articles at *www.spectra.blog*. The experiences described here may not be the case for all autists; however the feedback the author has received indicates that knowing our own autistic functionality patterns and challenges is very useful. One online follower said of this content: *'This is the greatest description I've seen of how my functioning fluctuates; I have such difficulty explaining it or even understanding it myself, so thank you for articulating it so well, and also for validating my experience.'* This chapter is written in the first person, e.g. 'What I have discovered...'.

When you are diagnosed as autistic, it takes a while to process everything if you were not previously aware that you were autistic. What I have come to believe is that, just as all autists are on an autism spectrum, we autists are also all on a 'spectrum within a spectrum'. And knowing your own autistic spectrum and functioning fluctuations is actually incredibly useful when it comes to self-care and mental wellbeing.

What I have discovered is that there are three main facets or divisions of my autism, which I liken to the red, amber and green colours of a traffic light; my 'green' days are my 'neutral' days, and the closest I get to being neurotypical (NT) or non-autistic. For me, I am 'green' for a good proportion of the time, if I maintain good self-care, and management of my social and sensory challenges. My 'red' days are what I would call my 'slow brain' days, when everything is challenging, and sensory overload is abundant. On these days, my 'bandwidth' is taken up with essential executive function, and the important elements of life, such as (in my case) parenting – there's no room for anything unimportant, like non-essential socialising. These are classed as red days as they're a cause for concern – I need to stop, assess, and utilise self-care; there's too much on my plate!

My 'amber' days are my 'fast brain' days; not necessarily a major cause for concern, as they're super-productive; and I achieve masses. But they're also something of a red flag, as they're mentally exhausting. I may for example need to assess and limit what I have planned the next day, to avoid going into 'red day' territory! But let me explain further. On my green days, I feel fairly 'typical' and as NT as I get; I'm not too tired, I don't feel especially antisocial, I am reasonably happy to see people and hold conversations and engage socially; and I can get quite a lot of pleasure out of life. (There's a sub-type of the green days that I would call 'neutral-slow' when I am feeling pretty good, but with a slight edge of irritation from excess visual and auditory stimulation).

My amber days (my 'superpower' days) generally happen once or twice a week; e.g. my fast brain days. In some ways, on these days, I am at my most autistic. In actual fact, I quite like them; it feels like my brain is supercharged; I'm multitasking on a massive level! I will for example write an article in my head (to be typed out later) whilst I am doing other things, e.g. cooking a meal; and it feels as if I have lots of metaphorical PC browser windows open in my head, all busily working. There are conversations, lists, plans, music etc. (Always music. The 'superpower' days usually have their own musical playlist on in the background. There is often a song on loop, or more usually, part of the song like the chorus, going around and around. I'm only now seeing this 'stuck record' as a little bit of a warning sign however; a sign that stress is building. Invariably, I have to find the song and listen to it later, to 'let it out'!)

On these amber days, I can however be irritated by how s-l-o-w-l-y other people (of any neurological persuasion!) are seemingly processing everything in their heads – especially in conversation, when my mind has moved on. On my 'superpower' days, I find that some people's brain-to-speech processing speed is often agonisingly slow. It annoys me when they want to focus or pontificate on something that my head processed and filed moments ago! This undoubtedly leads to me appearing bossy and short-fused. It's like telling someone you're taking the M25 motorway to somewhere, and your friend wants to s-l-o-w-l-y talk about every possible junction number and A-road, en-route. *"Move on! My brain has covered that…"* I fume, internally. (It is OK though; I may be smugly fast-processing on these amber days. But on my red days, I sometimes feel like I am barely functioning. Then, it's other people's turn to become frustrated at my own processing limitations).

I hadn't realised that these 'superpower' amber days often precede my slow (red) brain days, when my brain is quite worn out; it seems you can't have one without the other. On these red days, I find it harder to communicate verbally and look people in the eye. Do you remember the old dial up internet systems? It feels as if this is my type of brain processor, on red days. I forget every-day words mid-conversation; I am tired, and often crave solitude; too much sensory input is massively annoying and even painful, to a degree. Some 'grating' sounds, like metal on concrete, are agonising, and hurt my teeth. Touch can be super-charged. Some supposedly quiet sounds, e.g. the rustling of a packet, or the sound of someone eating, may seem deafening. So why are these slow brain days categorised as red?

Because this is a big warning that some self-care is needed. Now's not the time to book a series of intensive work meetings, or socialise in large groups. This is a time when some quietitude, some favourite music on the headphones, and plenty of sleep are in order. Generally, these slow brain days only last a day (or maybe two, if I wasn't able to look after myself and reduce sensory/social input on the first day).

But what's next, if as an autistic a person on a 'slow brain day', you can't administer self-care – or if you continue to push yourself (or have to push yourself because of work) over the course of a few of these 'slow brain' days? It's the dreaded shutdown. (See the chapter: *'S is for shutdown'*). Essentially, to continue the computing analogy, autistic shutdown can be described as feeling like a PC that's not equipped with update software – it simply has too many apps, browsers or programmes open. Autistic shutdown (in this author's opinion and experience) is short-term self-preservation mode, from a mental and emotional perspective. It's when you need to start closing down your programmes, to conserve energy, and generally, only the most important programme (which may be the 'parent programme'), is left on. Everything else closes down to a degree, just to conserve your own battery life – as if you keep going at your current level, you will become unwell. Therefore, red days are categorised as such because if the autistic challenges (especially sensory) are not dealt with, shutdown beckons. And if the individual is still unable to recalibrate, autistic burnout could ensue – see the chapter: *'B is for burnout'* – something this author sees as a more serious and longer-lasting state; a physiological response to emotional shutdown.

The autist's view

Having noted how I felt for the purpose of the original online article (the contents of which are included in this book chapter), an average week for me looked like:

Day 1 – Fast brain (amber).

Day 2 – Slow brain (red).

Day 3 – Neutral/slow (green).

Day 4 – Neutral (green).

Day 5 – Neutral (green).

Day 6 – Neutral/slow (green).

Day 7 – Neutral (green).

(Although after a 'good' week like this, I can be pretty sure that a fast brain day is due).

However, as an update to my original online article, I am now intrigued by the amount of green days that I experienced when I wrote it – in a different week, I think I may see more amber and even red days. This just shows that every day and every week is different for us autists. Also, I have noted that fast brain or amber days usually signal poor sleep that night. If other autists can also identify such patterns, they may be able to pre-empt 'poor sleep' nights, perhaps by meditations, herbal sleep remedies, quiet evenings, etc.

One follower of my original online article usefully commented: 'I am newly [diagnosed] and have noticed that there has been a pattern of lifelong periods of differences in function. I have [now] begun to track my days of extreme non-function, and noticed that hyper-sensory overload was non-stop. I spent 50 years mistaking sensory problems for a mysterious mental illness. I didn't know that other people [autistic individuals] also had these problems, and neither did my parents or my teachers or my doctors. I will now track all of my days and see if I can distinguish a pattern. I think I've been in a melt/shut down/recover/repeat cycle, and I think I can ameliorate some of my difficulties, now that I know where to dig for solutions.'

L is for
labels and language

If you are the parent of a child that you think may be autistic, you will almost definitely get asked the question: *'But why would you want to give him/her a label?'*

There are different kinds of labels, where autism is concerned – firstly, let's look at what the word 'label' means. People tend to use the word, as in the above example, when they think that being given a clinical diagnosis gives you some kind of stigma, or disadvantage. However, in this author's mind, an autism diagnosis is that – a diagnosis, not a label – it means the individual meets a specific, clinically-agreed set of criteria for a condition, and this in turn means that the diagnosed individual may have access to support and services. There are certainly some frustrating connotations surrounding autism, due to a lack of understanding and education, and that is probably where the fear of so-called labelling comes in.

Let's now look at the (now dated) functioning labels: 'high func-tioning' and 'low functioning'. These are rarely used clinically now, but are still in the autism vernacular. These terms have been used by parents and clinicians predominantly, to describe an autistic individual. As an example, traditionally someone with an Asperger's-type diagnosis would be described as having high functioning autism, and someone who is non-verbal or maybe has intellectual disabilities would have been described as low functioning. Thankfully these descriptions are clinically 'out of the window', now. Diagnostically, autism is autism, and instead of being described as high or low functioning, an autistic individual can be described as having support needs which are high or low; this is more acceptable language. In terms of these functioning labels, if you were the autistic individual who was termed 'high functioning', for some individuals, it was like being given some kind of patronising badge: *It's okay, you're not low functioning; in fact, you're not far off being normal!* (And this type of ableist language is still being bandied about, sadly).

But using these labels presented two problems. Problem one: your so-called lower functioning autistic friends and peers were made to feel inferior. They may have additional learning and processing challenges, or difficulties with verbal communication (for example), meaning that outsiders believe the autistic person is functioning at a so-called 'lower' level. However, the autistic individual's 'functionality' shouldn't be defined by a perceived deficit in one communication style, or the way they fit into a predefined infrastructure, or environment.

Problem two: as a supposed high functioning autist, your own struggles and challenges were not recognised. Remember, autism is widely said to be a processing difference, at its core – and how an individual is perceived to 'function' on a given day in a given environment by third parties is surely not a clinical description; more an observational one? As we explain in the chapter: *'M is for masking'*, autists are often very capable of masking to fit in, but this doesn't necessarily reflect their internal struggles and emotional energy levels.

In fact, there have been clear divisions within the autistic community concerning labels, for example with some family members of individuals diagnosed as being 'classically' autistic questioning whether someone with Asperger's was 'truly' autistic or 'autistic enough'. The more recent use of autism as a single diagnostic term is surely a step forward, to combat these divisions. It should be pointed out that high functioning and low functioning are still often used as descriptive terms, and this author concedes that there can be an occasional benefit to their use, in context, to help understanding, as they are phrases that people are used to. However, with education, hopefully once people understand that autism is predominantly an issue of processing (and that it's the co-existing conditions that the autistic may (or may not) have, alongside their autism, that tend to affect their support needs), the functioning labels will die out.

It is worth mentioning the further (also dated) terms 'mild' and 'severe', when used to describe autism. These equated to high and low functioning autism respectively, and are sometimes still used in the media, when describing someone who has autism – notably someone with high support needs e.g. 'severe autism'. It is the author's perception that again, 'severe' and 'mild' are not very helpful terms, and 'has high support needs' and 'has low support needs' are better phrases to be used. One issue to consider is that in cases where 'severe' is used to describe an individual's autism, it seems unlikely that the individual themselves has a say in how they're being described. The vast majority of autists are able to communicate somehow, and if it is not through verbalisation, then there are various communication devices, as well as writing and typing, that would allow the autistic person some input into the language that's used to describe them.

Next, let's consider the language used to describe someone who is autistic, which consistently causes division and differing opinions. Do we use identity first language e.g. Jane is autistic, or person first language, e.g. Jane has autism? There is no correct answer here, and opinion seems to be fairly evenly split – some autistic individuals prefer to say they 'have' autism, presumably because they don't want their autism to define their identity –

e.g. it is just a part of their overall make up. Conversely, other individuals prefer to say that they are autistic, because they believe that their autism affects, informs and defines so many areas of their life, and is their intrinsic being.

Person first language is the older (and possibly more out-dated?) phrasing, and apparently, according to America's National Center on Disability and Journalism, stems from America's re-named Individuals With Disabilities Education Act, which replaced the Education for All Handicapped Children Act in 1990. Critics of person first language in terms of autism believe it separates the person from the autism, when in fact, this is impossible to do. An autist can't take off their autism, like a hat! The best course of action is often just to ask an autist how they like to be described, or even just listen and watch, and you will hear the language they use. The website of the Autistic Self Advocacy Network has a useful article. (See: *www.tiny.cc/ASAN*). The site contains more useful links and articles on the subject of person first or identity first language.

One frustrating element of autistic labelling and language is when parents of autistic children describe the children in a certain way, for example 'severely autistic' or 'low functioning'. It seems to take away some autonomy and identity from the child. (The icing on the cake is when the parent describes themselves as an 'Autism Parent'! There are many T-shirts emblazoned with 'Autism Mom / Autism Mum', as a case in point. Surely they're just a parent? The autism community tends to find the 'Autism Parent' terminology a little patronising and leaning into martyrdom, as if the parent is owning the identity, when they don't necessarily need to, unless they're autistic too).

A further term falling within the bracket of autism labels and language is 'aspie', e.g. someone who has a diagnosis of Asperger Syndrome (or self-identifies). Since the decline of the term

'Asperger Syndrome', 'Aspie' is being used less, however. Also, there are the terms 'autist' or 'autie', to describe someone who is autistic; all perfectly acceptable when used descriptively, and not unkindly.

The autist's view

You can see from these sections within the book that I use the phrase 'autist', and also sometimes 'aspie', comfortably so. My belief is that when talking about one's own autism, or talking about somebody else who is autistic, while it might take a little longer to gain understanding and clarity, avoiding phrases like mild or severe, and not using functioning labels, is a more beneficial way to move forward. Even though it may take a little longer to educate people about what is meant!

I often get asked about the term 'high functioning', and try to explain to people that it is a perceived position of functionality in the environment, rather than a description of someone's autistic functionality. There are many examples of autistic individuals previously deemed as 'low functioning' (who may communicate in different, non-verbal ways), who have created great works of creativity, from art to literature, illustrating that they're far from low functioning.

In terms of person or identify first language, I realise that identity first is increasingly preferred, but I do think that the 'split' of opinion is slim. If someone chooses not to be defined by their autism (e.g. identifies as having autism, instead of being autistic), that's fine by me. I find it interesting that ADHD doesn't face similar heated debates, e.g. the English language almost forces us to say: 'She has ADHD.' (Some parents describe their child as 'an ADHD-er' which is a nice compromise). From a personal perspective, I do try to write using identity first, e.g. 'is autistic'. Autism is a constant filter through which we experience the world, and as an autist, we're never 'not autistic', and we can't take it off like a hat that's 'with' us. But at the time of writing, I genuinely don't mind, and wouldn't take offence at being described as 'having autism'.

Here's another aspie point of view. (Remember, I personally don't have a problem with describing myself in this way.) One of the followers of our source blog, *www.spectra.blog*, told this author: 'The term 'high functioning' is an injustice, as someone with a half decent IQ who cannot manage basic daily life, to the extent it has precluded my success in more demanding areas of which I am more than capable. The fact that it [high functioning] refers only to a lack of intellectual disability is lost, since its common meaning is, 'able to manage just fine thanks', which certainly is not the case just because a person can grasp concepts, and read. Perhaps [the term] 'autism' should not be assumed to include intellectual disability.'

L is for learning styles

It is important to consider how we learn (from a sensory perspective), and how autists' sensory challenges affect this. The primary or dominant learning styles of all individuals are said to use the three main sensory receivers: visual, auditory, and kinaesthetic – the latter is essentially learning by doing, and includes 'tactile' learning – e.g. a physical type of learning.

Essentially, all individuals use memory and perception to learn – and these two elements are often different in autists. All of us use all of the three main learning styles to a degree, however we do tend to have a preference for one. Very young children are generally taught (in an educational setting) using movement-based methods; older children's teaching is often more visually presented; and for senior students, including those moving into college education, auditory learning is more usual. Good teachers would presumably use a blend of teaching techniques, and recognise individuals' dominant learning styles, and adapt the learning as required.

Helping identify an autist's dominant learning style can help an autistic child access their education, and could reduce stress. As an example, a young autistic boy this author knows, aged six, struggles (as a kinaesthetic learner) to remember a text he has to read at school, which is then directly followed by a comprehension question – all read by the boy on paper. He could be greatly helped by teaching techniques that involve touching, building, moving, or drawing a subject, in order to learn about it. He may also find it beneficial to hold something (like a fidget pen or toy, which can be tapped or held), while learning, to disperse some energy and aid focus. One point that this author has been pondering is whether our dominant learning style is also our Achilles heel, as an autistic. For example, I am an auditory learner – I say things out loud to learn them, can recall information by simply hearing it, and work comfortably with sound in the background. However my dominant autistic sensory challenges are also auditory. On a sensitive day, it is sounds, chattering, people's mouth or eating noises, background noise, 'grating' noises like metal on concrete etc, that challenge my system the most.

So, it is as if my auditory system is amplified – and this not only allows me to effectively learn through auditory means, but also brings my system down when my auditory processing is overloaded. I can only speak as an autist and not for anyone else of a neurotypical (NT or non-autistic) persuasion, but if other autists experience this 'ying and yang' issue too, identifying it could be most beneficial, in terms of helping an autistic child access learning.

The Autism Research Institute gives some examples of how autistic children may learn as follows (also see: *www.tiny.cc/learning_styles*):

> If an autistic child enjoys looking at books (e.g. picture books), watching television (with or without sound), and tends to look carefully at people and objects, then he/she may be a visual learner.

> If an autistic child talks excessively, enjoys people talking to him/her, and prefers listening to the radio or music, then he/she may be an auditory learner.

And if an autistic child is constantly taking things apart, opening and closing drawers, and pushing buttons, this may indicate that the child is a kinaesthetic or 'hands-on' learner. The organisation states: '*It is important that educators assess for learning style as soon as an autistic child enters the school system and that they adapt their teaching styles in rapport with the strengths of the student.*'

Of course, not all learning takes place at school, and the same theories can be replicated at home. It really does make sense to work to a child's strengths rather than 'squash' them into a learning methodology that doesn't 'fit' them!

The autist's view

As someone who returned to study later in life (initially to study autism), it had been a while since I had given much thought to my own learning style. I am aware of my own child's learning style, and we instinctively use methods that support it. So it has been useful thinking about to what degree a particular dominant sense works for or against us, as autists! I am currently continuing my own studies, and will endeavour to utilise the many video and audio resources to enhance my learning, as a predominantly auditory learner.

M is for masking

Autists commonly experience difficulties in key areas including communication, socialisation and sensory challenges. It's also common for autists to experience emotional rigidity and repetitive thought processes or behaviours. Looking at the areas of socialisation and communication especially, it becomes clearer why many autistic individuals, (subconsciously or otherwise), end up masking – e.g. presenting oneself differently in one's behaviour, in order to hide certain traits, or mimic neurotypical (NT or non-autistic) behaviours. So, masking (or camouflaging / passing) is a way of 'fitting in' and meeting people's expectations.

Masking may sound quite superficial, but it is in fact necessary to get through the day for most autists; for example, earning a wage in order to feed the family, fitting in at work, meeting social conventions and carrying out the required workplace tasks (often without relevant support). In places of education, this 'fitting in' is usually required in order to access the education on offer without confrontation or revealing one's struggles, as well as to meet social conventions, potentially avoid punishments, and avoid standing out or being ostracised or bullied. In everyday life, masking may be required a lot of the time to simply achieve life's supposedly important social requirements; e.g. chatting to a cashier at the supermarket, being friendly towards the neighbours, or mingling at a family function. That is not to say that the autistic individual doesn't want to be friendly, and chat to the cashier, neighbour or family member – just that this very action takes a lot of mental processing, and energy units. Autism is after all at its core a difference in processing, so every interaction for the autist takes up energy units. If the autistic individual had a completely full tank of energy units, then chatting to the cashier, family member or neighbour would probably not represent such a problem. But if most of the energy units have been allocated with daily executive functioning, there's very little processing data available, making communication of any kind an effort.

Rather than simply seeing Mary the neighbour and having a chat that requires no effort, the energy-depleted autist is likely to be going through a mental tick list as they see the neighbour. *'Who is that? It's Mary. I need to say hello to Mary. Should I ask her how her pet is? What's her pet's name? Will she say hello to me first?'* Each thought process takes mental and processing effort – the autist may even rehearse the conversation in his or her head as they approach, to make sure it sounds appropriate. Remember, they're doing this for the neighbour's benefit, not for their own. How exhausting! The autist's natural (and probably preferred) state would be not to say hello on this occasion, to just go home and recalibrate after the day's challenges. But in order to meet social convention, the autist will probably be friendly, and try to 'pass' as a neurologically-appropriate individual.

Multiply this effort dozens of times each day, and we see that due to the autist's differences in processing and communication, interacting with other people can be draining. Hence a 'mask' is used to appear NT, or to simply pass as a functional individual who's following social convention. Remember, this isn't a reflection on the autist's desire to interact with the other person – the autist may very much want to communicate with them – it's simply relative to the amount of mental processing required to do so, when the energy bank is already depleted from processing everything else in the environment at that time. (E.g. the bright sunlight, the din of background noise on the bus, and the busy neighbourhood).

Autistic masking doesn't just take place with non-family members – autists may mask around their close friends, spouses, parents, children and other family members too, not because they can't be themselves, but because they love their close friends and family members so much that they don't want to cause concern and make the family member worry that there's something wrong. Maybe the autist, if feeling low, anxious or tired, just wants to appear as the best version of themselves? Like maximising your appearance, putting on a smarter outfit, or putting on make-up. In an ideal world, no masking would be required around loved ones. A family member, knowing their autistic loved one had just done the school run, returned from the office, been shopping or had generally had a tiring day, would recognise a beleaguered expression, and knowingly stick their thumb up with a smiling, enquiring face, to silently question, '*Are you ok?*' And the autist would smile and stick their thumb up to silently reply, '*Yes, I'm okay, thank you for understanding and pre-empting my mental exhaustion, spoon depletion and social hangover, but I'm just not up to talking right now, or at least not taking about non-essential things.*' And all would be well. But families aren't all like that, are they! It's perhaps simply a matter of education and awareness, however. (See the chapters: '*H is for hangover (social)*', and '*S is for spoons theory*' for more information on energy units).

It's important to note that young children don't have that awareness of their parents' sensitivities, as described above – so the run-down autistic parent is quite likely to mask and appear engaged and energised while they're 'parenting', so as not to concern their child. Hence, the autist may mask to make their families feel happy, often at their own expense, not because they're unhappy about being themselves, but because they care. It's also worthwhile mentioning childhood masking, specifically. Autistic women are said to mask more than men, and it would seem that autistic girls mask more than boys. Masking is a way of navigating reality – remember, it may be subconscious – and for autistic girls, it's a valuable tool to fit in with peers. But successful masking can lead outsiders to be so convinced of the individual's 'typicality' that their autism goes unnoticed. Additionally, it's common for a child (of either gender) to 'mask' at school and 'let it all out' when they return home to the safety of their own surroundings, and people who 'get' them. The website Spectrum News, reporting on a study, states: '[Researchers found that] boys with autism might be overactive or appear to misbehave, whereas girls more often seem anxious or depressed.' (See: www.tiny.cc/masking_gender).

It is also interesting to note that masking can include the hiding of self-stimulatory behaviours (stims – see the chapter: 'S is for stimming'), like fidgeting or tapping. The autistic individual may bite their cheek, clench their fists or flex and relax a muscle – all things that probably go unnoticed, but help to self-regulate the autist. In summary, autistic masking in small measures is maybe not bad thing, to help one's self esteem, and feel like less of an outsider. However, too much masking, which can occur long-term when the autist is not yet diagnosed as being autistic, can be hugely depleting; it is also thought to be associated with mental health challenges like anxiety and depression. Once autism diagnosis occurs, it does also throw up the question, who's the real me? And too much masking can lead to social hangovers, shutdown and autistic burnout. (See the relevant chapters on these subjects). It could be said that getting the balance right between self-care and being true to one's autistic-self, as well as fitting into a predominantly NT society and masking along the way, is the eternal holy grail for most autistic individuals.

The autist's view

The detrimental effects of masking are seriously under-estimated, in my opinion. NT individuals who are able to communicate naturally and without too much forethought whatever their mental states (e.g. tiredness, sadness etc) may not be able to imagine the effort an autist has to make, simply to navigate a normal social environment like a school. Add something like anxiety into the mix, and masking is the only option available in order to 'fit in'; something that is often done for others' benefit, rather than one's own. Masking is said to be a major reason why many individuals' autism is picked up late, and this is a desperate shame for undiagnosed children, when simple supports in school could be given once teachers know a child is struggling and masking to 'hide' their natural responses.

M is for meltdown

Meltdown describes the situation where the individual – autistic or otherwise, as it is not only a term used for neurominorities – is no longer able to cope. Their skillsets aren't sufficiently honed to deal with the situation at that time, and the individual lets off steam one way or another, in order to recalibrate. (Skillsets may include social and language skills, as well as executive functioning skills, as examples). Autistic meltdowns differ from person to person, and some autistic individuals, especially adults, say that they rarely have meltdowns. (They will undoubtedly experience challenges and periods of 'overwhelm', but perhaps they head straight to shutdown (see the chapter: 'S is for shutdown'), or some kind of low mood, or withdrawal).

Meltdowns can sometimes be defined as panic attacks; they may look like tantrums; sometimes they can just be bursts of anger or frustration, and they can manifest as tears or extreme sadness. They may be over extremely quickly once the individual has let off steam, or they may last for a much longer duration. On some occasions, a meltdown is extremely serious, as the individual or people in close proximity may be at risk, e.g. from violent or erratic behaviour. Some experts describe meltdowns as 'neural high jacking', when coherent, rational thought is absent, and what is left is a debilitated state of incoherence. According to psychologist Dr. Daniel Goleman, what the child does and says during meltdown is simply 'mental debris'. (Visit: *www.danielgoleman.info*). Sometimes (as an outsider), one can see a meltdown coming, in an autist; and in fact a teacher or carer may even want to want the meltdown to occur, simply so the child can recalibrate, and get the outpouring over and done with in a safe and supportive space. The teacher may for example spot signs in the classroom, such as the child being easily upset, 'spoiling for a fight' or picking an argument, having a lot of nervous energy, or generally becoming withdrawn. There could be specific rituals or behaviours that the child is doing ahead of the meltdown; maybe for example an anxiety-related stim (see the chapter: '*S is for stimming*') like clenching and releasing the teeth, or clicking their fingers. Or, the child may have the self-awareness to realise a meltdown is imminent, and recognise triggers. (As do many adults).

The meltdown triggers themselves are many and varied; they obviously vary depending on the individual and are usually multifactorial. Elements like sensory overload from sources like lights and noise may play a part (clinicians may describe this as 'sensory integration dysfunction'); as well as excessive demands (or things that are perceived to be demands by the autistic individual). Excessive socialisation, known stressful situations, and anything that triggers the autist's quirks or 'peccadillos' (e.g. maybe a favourite food has run out, or a planned play date has been cancelled), can contribute to meltdowns.

It is often said that masking is a factor for meltdowns too; masking or trying to appear 'typical' can be very energy depleting. (See the chapter: '*M is for masking*'). Whether it is trying to fit in at school, attempting to follow social conversations in a group, or blending in with neurotypical (NT or non-autistic) colleagues in the workplace, the act of masking one's autism drains emotional energy, or conceptual 'mental bandwidth'. A build-up of masking, combined with general tiredness and a specific trigger, however minor it is perceived to be, can easily trigger autistic meltdowns.

Therefore, some or all of the triggers described above (as well as others not listed, but relative to the individual) can initiate meltdown. Other everyday factors like tiredness and hunger, as well as hormones, can also play a part. Often, the concept of 'the straw that broke the camel's back' can take place, e.g. something that seems innocuous and not worthy of such a level of upset can tip one over the emotional edge – the proverbial last straw. It is not uncommon for autistic children educated at school to meltdown at home, after a day of blending in, and masking at school – invariably, they are melting down in their safe place, even though the anxiety was building all day. This can lead to parents' concerns about the possibility of an autism diagnosis for their child to be questioned by educators and outsiders, as those who do not understand the challenges presented by autism may assume the cause of the meltdown is just occurring 'at home'. In such instances, viewpoints like: 'Well, she seems fine at school', or 'Maybe he's picking up on the parents' anxiety at home,' are rarely helpful.

The main challenges presented by autism – difficulties communicating and socialising, sensory challenges (e.g. to noise and light, for example), and specific thinking styles or rigid thought processes that aren't supported by the learning style at the school – can all cause great anxiety to a child. (See the chapter: 'L is or learning styles'). It's no wonder that after a day of using up all of their emotional energy units or 'spoons', many autistic kids come home and feel comfortable enough to let their frustrations and emotions out. (The reference to spoons relates to the spoons theory, a kind of disability metaphor developed by Christine Miserandino, who has lupus, and uses 'spoons' to explain how to ration one's energy. See the chapters: '*H is for hangover (social)*' and '*S is for spoons theory*').

Different individuals react differently – some may meltdown in the more obvious sense, e.g. excessive stimming, tears, anger, arguments and even out-of-control aggression, while others may consciously try to make their meltdown more low key, and private. (The latter is potentially a big concern, as self-harming could be an issue). For the loved one, educator or carer of an autist, the key to coping with meltdowns is often to get a handle on what triggers that individual, to help reduce factors that are likely to trigger the meltdown. Once the meltdown has started, it really needs to run its course – it is, after all, a release, a situation of overwhelm, or a kind of panic attack. Naturally, it is best not to judge or be cross about the meltdown. Sometimes the individual may appreciate someone being close to them (e.g. in the room, or outside the door); other times, they may need or prefer to be left alone, to work through the process. Once the autist has calmed down (and when they're ready, which may even be the next day), the family member, carer or educator may find the opportunity to talk about what happened, what triggered the episode, and how everyone handled it. Generally, autists in meltdown are unable to discuss anything properly at the time, as their emotional bandwidth is busy trying to recalibrate, and manage their 'fight or flight' response. Directly afterwards, they may feel too exhausted to talk. (NB – some families do have to cope with very aggressive and even dangerous meltdowns, and at these times, keeping all individuals safe is the priority. See the information on interventions for meltdowns, below).

Dr. Ross Greene has studied and written extensively about what he describes as the 'inflexible-explosive child', and has written a book titled: The Explosive Child (HarperCollins – see: *www.tiny.cc/Ross_Greene*), full of fascinating facts and tips.

Rebecca Law, American advocate for autistic children and their families, states in her paper (based on Dr. Green's concepts): 'Thoughtful response to agitation, escalation and meltdowns in children with autism spectrum disorders' (see: *www.tiny.cc/rebeccaklaw*): *'Inflexible and explosive children have difficulty managing and controlling emotions associated with frustration. They also have difficulty thinking through ways of resolving frustrating situations. In these children, frustration (usually caused by a demand to 'shift gears') often leads to a state of cognitive debilitation'.*

Her paper, based on Dr. Ross Greene's work, details useful de-escalation techniques, including the tip to offer words that describe the mounting feelings. (E.g. *"I know you are really mad that it is time to go! It is hard to stop playing with that toy. I understand."*) Green and Law also advocate framing requests (e.g. from the parent or educator to the child) as either A, B or C requests, with A being vital and non-negotiable (e.g. taking crucial medication), and C being not terribly important (e.g. wearing a warm hat).

Law also includes this invaluable gem, which is aimed at the person who is addressing the autistic child who is in meltdown: *'You need to stop talking, unless your words have a soothing effect [on the autistic individual].'* Many families of autistic individuals, and autists themselves, say that using movement often helps disperse feelings associated with meltdown. Therefore, having a trampoline to 'bounce out' feelings can help, as can activities linked to pressure (e.g. pressing one's hands against a wall, lying heavily over a Swiss ball, or lying under a weighted blanket, as examples).

A word on interventions for meltdowns – it may be useful, in more relaxed situations, to discuss with the autist their preferences for how their families or their educators 'deal' with future meltdowns. (The meltdown could be given a different name, if it is too accusatory, e.g. overwhelm, or a childish phrase like fizzy brain or volcano time, that the child perhaps helps to choose. Drawing how it feels could help to name it).

As a last resort, modest physical interventions may be required to retain safety, e.g. if de-escalation techniques haven't worked – these physical interventions would be classed as restricting an individual's movement, liberty or freedom to act independently – e.g. restricting access, or physically holding them somehow. The National Autistic Society (NAS) states that almost everyone who is autistic has the ability to express a view on how they'd like to be treated, so consent for potential restraining actions should ideally be sought. (NICE, the National Institute for Health & Care Excellence, advises – *'Restrictive interventions should only be used if all attempts to diffuse the situation have failed, and the individual becomes aggressive or violent.'* (See: *www.nice.org.uk*).

The autist's view

It's worth as an autistic individual trying to work out one's own triggers for meltdown – especially if it involves the more private meltdown, that could include self-harm (which could include self-medicating with alcohol for example, or controlling food intake). Having the self-awareness to see when one is out of 'spoons', is feeling anxious, and could be triggered into meltdown, is a very valuable skillset to have! Keeping items to hand that would be useful if oneself or a family member is trying to manage feelings connected to meltdown (maybe beloved soft toys, weighted blankets, headphones and preferred music, etc) is also a useful way to manage the feelings – as is retreating to a safe place to mentally recalibrate, away from triggers and sensory challenges.

As a parent, it is easy to get pulled into arguments with children (of any neurology), and to (perhaps because of traditional parenting methods which have a perceived need to be superior, or to have the last word) keep talking, or berate a child that's showing behaviour that challenges. However, stopping talking as the adult or carer in the situation is a great lesson to learn. There are always basic signs (as in sign language) that can be utilised when someone's too upset to talk, even a thumbs up or down, and staying silent instead of saying what first comes to mind can be so useful, and can allow a child to process something by themselves. This is why I loved Rebecca Law's blunt advice for the person who is addressing an autistic child who is in meltdown: "You need to stop talking, unless your words have a soothing effect." Another great phrase is 'Connection before correction', e.g. to use to avoid getting pulled into arguments with children.

M is for music

One of this author's most popular online articles on *www.spectra.blog* has been on the subject of music, and whether (some) autists feel music differently. This chapter is quite a personal one, written about the author's own experiences.

Like the vast majority of the population, I really enjoy music. I'd like to discuss here how music makes us feel. I can only speak as an autist, as I only know how music feels to me; and I don't know to what degree what I feel is the same for other neurodivergent people, or indeed for neurotypical (NT) people across the population. As rather than just listening to and enjoying music, I feel it. Before delving further into this chapter however, I will highlight an interesting article I read, called *'If Music Gives You Goosebumps, You May Have A Very Special Brain'*. (See: *www.tiny.cc/specialbrain*). It reports that: *'People who get a reaction from music make an emotional and physical connection to the sounds they're hearing... [and] actually have a different brain structure to people who don't. The fibres that connect the auditory cortex (the part that processes everything you hear) and the areas that process emotion have a denser volume [in people that feel and 'react' to music, as opposed to ...] people who feel nothing at all.'* This article leads me to believe that (a) not everyone feels or interprets music in the way that myself and many other people do, and (b) there could be a very real chance that (some) autistic brains have different auditory fibres, giving the autist a very different experience of listening to music.

So for me, as an autist, most of all I think I like to feel the bass. You simply can't beat a good bass drum or a good bass guitar (and preferably both); a nice way to experience this is at a live gig, and often the louder the better – this is quite a physical feeling, in terms of the beat going through your body. It is also great to feel and interpret music when listening to it at home, ideally via good-quality headphones. As an autist, e.g. with the autistic trait of challenges in processing emotions, music changes the way I am feeling in an extremely fast way – with a mechanism that can over-ride usual emotional processing speeds. For me, it isn't necessarily about the lyrics; these may count of course, but it is more the key of the music, the timbre of the voice, and the emotional tone of the piece. One of the best ways to illustrate this is with a song: 'I Believe (When I fall in love with you it will be forever)' by Stevie Wonder. It is in my opinion one of the best pop songs ever written. (Art Garfunkel's version is my favourite). The key changes at: *'The many sounds that meet our ears, the sights our eyes behold... will open up our merging hearts and feed our empty souls,'* and a stringy, uber-emotional pre-chorus bridge lifts you up into the chorus. It's unrivalled in my mind. Just that sixteen-second piece of music (the bridge!) brings me to tears sometimes, not because of sadness, but because it is so moving.

This is a romantic song of course, so it makes sense that it's been created in order to 'move' us. But more upbeat (and / or non-romantic themes) can have a similar effect. If I'm feeling particularly sensitive from an autistic sensory point of view, then good 'bassy' music works well. Robert Plant, in some of his more recent works, has used African drum rhythms and a type of drum called a 'bendir', and literally hearing one or two of these drum beats on a song of his that I enjoy can fill me with uplifting emotion. The timbre of someone's voice can give me goose bumps, and again this is not necessarily about the words they are singing – a good example of a voice conveying emotion is George Michael. *'The first time ever I saw her face'*, originally sung by Peggy Seeger and made famous by Roberta Flack, is sung beautifully on George's Symphonica album. Although the words are beautiful, it is the sound of his voice and the intent of his words, e.g. his emotional delivery based on his own experiences and the person he's singing it to, that makes this version especially spine tingling.

Another thing I enjoy doing is picking apart a song – for example, on one hearing, listening to vocalist A's voice, and then re-playing and focussing on vocalist B's voice. (Modern country vocal groups are often great for this, due to their harmonies and layered production). And I like identifying the different instruments on a song, and perhaps working out who is playing them. Sometimes in music documentaries, you can find out interesting things about items used in recording sessions to create a sound (like coins, boxes or a bicycle bell), or a unique setting or room that created a specific recording ambience. The 'wall of sound' techniques employed by Brian Wilson and The Wrecking Crew session musicians on the iconic Pet Sounds Beach Boys album are really worth a listen, to pick out all of the innovative elements and world-class musicians. My point of discussion is: are these feelings and interpretations of mine linked to being autistic, and if so; how amazing! In my opinion, many well-known musicians, singers and songwriters seemingly have traits of autism, even if the artist themselves is unaware that they may be autistic, or at the very least has not 'come out' as being autistic. The fact that many musicians seemingly have autistic traits is probably because autism can bring great creativity, and a fascination with word play, particularly rhyming, and also a dedication to learning, possibly linked to repetitive thought processes. This surely lends itself to learning a musical instrument, or honing one's voice with hours of practice.

NB – there are some interesting studies linked to autism and music – one titled *'Neural systems for speech and song in autism'*, published in the journal 'Brain', concludes that: *'In autism, functional systems that process speech and song were more effectively engaged for song than for speech.'* (See: *www.tiny.cc/speech_song*). Interestingly, many autists are said to have synaesthesia, when one sense automatically triggers another, e.g. seeing a sonic colour palette and experiencing colours when hearing musical pieces and notes. Musicians including Lorde, Billy Joel, Dev Hynes, Thom York and Pharrell Williams have described this experience. Discussing her album Melodrama with Ryan Seacrest, Lorde explained how she sees sounds and words as colours. *"Making music is very visual for me. I can see it. Sometimes it can be really overwhelming colour-wise, and we'll have to sort of dial it back through the music,"* she said – see: *www.tiny.cc/syn_lorde*).

Pharrell Williams told Maureen Seaberg, for a book titled Tasting the Universe – "There are seven basic colors: red, orange, yellow, green, blue, indigo and violet. And those also correspond with musical notes. White, believe it or not, which gives you an octave, is the blending of all the colors. Colors are light in the electromagnetic spectrum. For every color, there is a sound, a vibration, a part of the human body, a number, a musical note." (See: *www.tiny.cc/syn_pharrell*). Billy Joel told Maureen Seaberg for the book Tasting the Universe of his synaesthesia: "I kind of like the spontaneity and the mystery of it all. It's very intriguing to me. My feeling is that all of this stuff exists in a different plane and we tap into it somehow, and I think I do it in a dream state." The singer also associates musical genres and word sounds, especially vowels, with colour. "When I have a particularly vivid color, it's usually a strong melodic, strong rhythmic pattern that emerges at the same time. When I think of certain songs, I think of vivid reds, oranges or golds." (See: *www.tiny.cc/syn_joel*). Some scientists believe that the visual areas of the brains of synesthetes (individuals with synaesthesia) are more active than non-synesthetes, with states of altered cortical wiring at the embryo stage. The theory is that auditory-visual synesthetes, e.g. those who can 'see' sounds' and vice versa, carry different variants of genes related to the development of neural connections. Put simply, their synaesthesia is just down to a different neurology; as is autism. A study published in the journal Science identified 'a handful' of genes that might predispose people to synaesthesia, explaining that the discovery may help scientists further understand autism. '[The study] provides a fascinating suggestion of a link between particular genetic variations and hyper-connectivity in the synesthetic brain,' Cognitive Psychologist Romke Rouw reported. (See: *www.tiny.cc/syn_autism*).

This link explains why this author has included extensive references to synaesthesia in an autism book. While synaesthesia is not specific to autism, it seems to be 'quite common' among autistic individuals, according to experts including Olga Bogdashina, Professor, Chief Research Fellow and Lecturer at the International Autism Institute. Professor Bogdashina reports that synaesthetes are observed to have uneven cognitive skills, are reported to prefer order, neatness, symmetry and balance, and are more prone to experiences such as déjà vu, right-left confusion (allochiria), and a poor sense of direction. (See: *www.tiny.cc/Bogdashina*). It seems clear to this author that synaesthesia is a fascinating form of neurodiversity – and with many autists experiencing sensory processing difficulties as part and parcel of their autism, the lines between synaesthesia and some of the facets of autism seem incredibly blurred.

The autist's view

This chapter has mostly been all about my view, so here's another autist's view, from one of the *www.spectra.blog* website followers, in response to the original online article about how I 'feel' music:

> "I listen to music that makes my neurons happy. I swear I can feel them firing when I hear a good song. Pop music doesn't usually do this, because it's so predictable. When I hear a song that surprises me and doesn't do what I expect, it makes me almost giddy. I would love to know what's happening in my brain. I imagine something akin to fireworks happening in there. I also know what you mean about deep bass sounds. When I hear bowed notes (as opposed to plucked) on an upright bass, it just floors me every time. It's such a rich sound that I feel in my chest. I always want to share my excitement about music with people in my life, but they don't seem to get the same feeling. I wish everyone could feel what I feel."

N is for neurodiversity

It is worth exploring what neurodiversity means, in the context of autism; to many people, it essentially represents the concept that autism is not a medical disability, but a difference in neurology – part of a diverse population. The term was first used by Judy Singer, an autistic social scientist, in a publication called The Atlantic, in 1998. She referred to it as a subset of biodiversity – diversity being a 'property of populations', not individuals. Ms. Singer described her term 'neurodiversity' as: *'An umbrella movement for any 'neurotribes' who had been stigmatised for having kinds of mind-bodies that were different from the largely imaginary normal'*, and by coining the phrase, explained that this was a way of *'conserving the diversity of the human species.'*

People who support the neurodiversity paradigm prefer to use autism spectrum neurology over words like disability and disorder – however, the various identifications and descriptions within the overall debate do lead to differences of opinion. At the time of writing, the term neurodiversity is often used in general parlance to mean those with cognitive differences, e.g. those who are neurologically-atypical – as opposed to its true meaning; a diverse neurological population. However, language by its nature does of course move on, and diversify! (Interestingly, Ms. Singer herself has recently stated that: *'Neurodiversity is not a synonym for neurological disability, divergence or difference'*. She reportedly now prefers the term 'neurominorities' for those with 'atypical cognition'. Source: *www.tiny.cc/JSinger*).

This author has stated throughout the book that autism is, at its core, widely considered to be a difference in processing. The neurodiversity movement generally believes that while clinical interventions for specific co-existing conditions or issues that cause challenges (like talking therapies for anxiety, speech therapies for language delay, or medications for epilepsy, as examples) are widely advocated, autism itself is not necessarily a disease or disorder. (It is worth remembering however that the UK's Equality Act and the Children And Families Act both class autism as a disability, as does the National Autistic Society – so anyone going through autism assessment, and issues connected to education or any local authority intervention or support, will likely come across the terms disorder and maybe disability, whether or not they use them within their own vocabulary). Let's consider some of the differences of opinion mentioned above, and why some individuals may have different viewpoints. For example, many individuals who are autistic, with few additional, co-existing conditions that are debilitating, and with minimal support needs, may not consider themselves to be disabled, or to have a disorder. They may simply identify as having autism spectrum neurology, or just to be autistic. After all, debilitating issues or traits (relating to socialisation and communication, as examples) could be seen to be only be 'disabilities' in that social context – in a different environment, they may cease to be a difficulty at all. Other individuals, most notably parents of autists, might argue that their son or daughter's autism is 'disabling', and does make the son or daughter feel 'disordered'. (Some autists themselves also feel this way). The way one feels about whether autism is a disability or not surely depends on one's own experiences and exposure to autism? Some parents of autists may support the medical paradigm (which can be seen as the opposite of the neurodiversity concept), because having a 'disorder' diagnosis can mean access to necessary support and services. Gaining an autism diagnosis can be a lengthy process, and sometimes the last thing on one's mind at this stage is vocabulary, and the distinctions of being in a neurominority, or differently-abled.

There is also the question hinted at above, of what makes one disabled – to what extent is it a social issue, in terms of access and infrastructure, as well as awareness? E.g. Is it a condition that disables you, or the lack of infrastructure and support in the community? If you go 'into' any social media support group consisting of autistic individuals and their families (and perhaps also to 'real life' social support groups; although these probably evoke more polite responses!), you will find a myriad of opinions on this subject. Often, when discussing the neurodiversity paradigm, people assume there is a wrong and a right, or a true and false, based on their own experiences of autism, when in fact we are all allowed an opinion on what autism is, and what it means to us. To reiterate, it simply depends on one's own experiences and exposure to autism. Some people also question what neurologies neurodiversity should include. For true diversity, all neurologies should be included, just as in the case of ethnic diversity, where all ethnicities are included – this was Judy Singer's view. However, if the online autism community is to be believed, some people seemingly want neurodiversity to be a select group; for example, to include autism and ADHD, but perhaps not dyslexia or dyspraxia. This author advocates that for true diversity, all neurologies should be included within the banner or umbrella.

Continuing the discussion over the use of the word disability versus the neurodiversity paradigm, there is also the issue of co-existing conditions to consider, in terms of whether it is these conditions that make one 'disordered' or disabled (or differently-abled). After all, autism is at its core said to be a processing difference; but would the addition of a further condition make one 'disabled' or 'dis-ordered'? (See also the chapter: 'C is for co-existing conditions'). Of course, it depends on the individual. It is also worth adding within this chapter that neurodiversity advocates are firmly against any behavioural 'therapies', training and interventions that are coercive in any way, and seek to make autists appear more neurotypical, or NT. (This aversion does not include conventional, respected therapies such as talking, play, speech and language and occupational therapies). The behavioural 'therapies' targeted at autistic individuals that alarm neurodiversity advocates so, seem to essentially seek to break down what the 'therapist' sees as either desirable or undesirable behaviours into repetitive steps, rewarding the autistic child for actions the 'therapist' deems appropriate. Some parents of autists may claim (while their offspring are still children) that the coercive behavioural training or 'therapy' they arranged for their autistic child has helped, or seen benefits; but this author remains to be convinced by a single autistic adult who has endured 'behavioural training' that such 'therapies' are in fact beneficial, rather than a system that's akin to teaching dogs obedience skills, or not to bark excessively. However, everyone is entitled to their opinions, and just because this author is unconvinced of the benefits of such 'therapy', others may disagree.

Moving back to the medical versus social paradigm – here's an interesting example of the medical paradigm, in terms of vocabulary. To compete as an autistic athlete under Para-athletic guidelines, one is considered to have an 'intellectual disability', as per guidelines in the International Paralympic Committee (IPC) Athletics Classification Handbook (see:

www.paralympic.org/ipc-handbook). (The definition here does talk about conceptual, social and practical adaptive skills; wording that does makes sense.) Intellectual disability is defined by the IPC as: *'A limitation in intellectual functioning and adaptive behaviour as expressed in conceptual, social and practical adaptive skills, which originates before the age of 18'*. (As in the case of British autistic swimmer Jessica-Jane Applegate MBE, classified as S14, e.g. a swimmer with an intellectual impairment – source: *www.tiny.cc/jessicaA*).

However, as we have discussed elsewhere, autism as a neurology does not necessarily equate to intellectual disability. Only around half of autists are thought to have intellectual or cognitive disabilities as well (see: *www.tiny.cc/mencap_autism*). One can see how problematic such semantics are for the International Paralympic committee, however! By virtue of the whole concept of the Paralympic movement (developed seventy years ago), people with 'physical, visual and intellectual disabilities' are considered eligible to compete against one another in their chosen sport. E.g. the para-athletic system is based on a medical disability model. Presumably if you are an autistic para-athlete labelled as having an intellectual disability, even if you don't consider yourself intellectually disabled, you accept the 'label' in order to compete in your sport, and focus more on the 'softer' description of having limitations in intellectual functioning and adaptive behaviour. Perhaps some of the issues concerning whether to embrace the neurodiversity paradigm or not stem from all autism profiles now being grouped together. When there were more functioning labels in use, it was perhaps easier for individuals to find their clan. Now that we (autists) are all in the same clan, trying to find common ground with other autists and their family members can be problematic, as the spectrum (and our individual experiences of autism) vary so much.

The autist's view

While I do massively support the neurodiversity paradigm, equally, the words disability and disorder don't offend me as an autist, if someone else uses them without malice. It is down to each individual, and their experiences shape their language. I don't actively consider myself to have a disability, but I can see why the National Autistic Society refers to autism as a disability as part of a social, political and legal model. I don't mind the abbreviation ASD (with D for disorder), but I understand that many followers of my writing prefer ASC (e.g. C for condition), or even more preferably, ASN (e.g. N for neurology). The term neurominority is a very acceptable one, I feel. However, I do think there is a good argument for sometimes including ASD and ASC as terms online. This is because with schools and clinicians using the terms, and the clinical studies that underpin a degree of our understanding of autism using medical terms like D for disability, providers of information need to make it easy to find online. If you are someone starting on your autism journey (as an individual, family member or professional), you want access to facts and information.

I wish there was less division within the autism community, especially between the parents of autists (who sometimes use terms like 'Autism Mom / Mum', which really riles autists, as this is akin to taking on the autist's identity, leading to allegations of 'martyr parenting'); and the autistics themselves. Furthermore, the idea of making neurodiversity a select club that only people of certain neurologies are eligible for is galling. I often get challenged on the language I use in writing (e.g. mentioning 'disorder') because an individual has a different opinion to me. But we are all entitled to our own opinions.

O is for obsession

One common trait among autists is hyper-focused interests or obsessions; this thinking style is now often thought of as monotropism, or 'atypical patterns of attention' (source: *www.tiny.cc/DMurray*). ('Hyper-focused interest' is however a nicer phrase than obsession, which does have negative connotations.) Repetitive behaviours and a propensity for sameness are after all key elements of autism, so it's no surprise that autists can become hyper-focussed on a subject. Autists tend to thrive on repetition and patterns, so anything with a regular element to it appeals to the autistic brain; for example collecting certain items. The 'collection' and 'special interest' elements often intertwine, meaning autists develop real expertise in their area of interest. (Collecting information can become an interest in itself; for example enjoying 'quizzing', like autist Anne Hegarty from UK TV's The Chase). Many autistics go on to become leading experts in their chosen field, and if extensive practise is required, for example to perfect a sporting discipline, again the autist's penchant for repetition serves them well. It's seemingly not uncommon for the interest to be slightly off-field or unusual however; in the eyes of neurotypical (NT) people especially.

So, what of the word obsession? This sometimes signifies the interest has reached unhealthy levels – but in whose eyes? There are many instances where a special interest (in someone of any neurology, not just in an autistic person), becomes unhealthy – one good example is obsessive computer gaming. Professor

Tony Attwood at his 2019 ACAMH 'What you need to know about Autism' presentation touched upon the subject, explaining that while computer gaming can be a tool to help cope with anxiety, and is a useful thought blocker, gaming can be very addictive. "Working with the individual before they get to an obsessive or addicted level is key. For autists who struggle with 'real world' socialisation, the non-face-to-face world of gaming can be very appealing," he explained. (A route to support expertise in gaming, or computing in general, is to embark on a career in the field. This allows the autistic individual to further their studies but keep up the interest. Thank goodness autist Satoshi Tajiri, creator of Pokemon, maintained his special teenage interest in arcade games, as he now has a very popular and successful business empire. Meanwhile, Silicon Valley in the USA is apparently awash with talented autistic individuals, and they're reportedly often specifically recruited).

Sometimes, obsessive behaviours can be detrimental to health and may lead to issues like unhealthy patterns (e.g. counting calories and eating disorders), in autists, or self-medicating with alcohol or drugs. Stereotypies like trichotillomania (hair pulling) and dermatillomania (skin picking) can also develop, which can be unhealthy. It is therefore important for families and friends to be vigilant for any mental health or repetitive / addiction-type issues, and involve relevant specialist clinicians and healthcare experts. Hyper-focussed interests can also extend to people, and this can also sometimes be unhealthy – e.g. forming an attraction or relationship that is unrequited. However, while obsessive behaviours can have negative connotations, for the most part, special interests (for someone of any neurology) are just that – a haven of safety and expertise. A joy; a feeling of validation; a sense of having found a tribe (of similar enthusiasts)! Autistic special interests are often cause for celebration. Professor Tony Attwood at his 2019 ACAMH

'What you need to know about Autism' presentation said that autistic special interests can be: A means of relaxation, pleasure; [a way of] using knowledge to overcome fear; [a way of] keeping anxiety under control; [a way of] thought blocking; an energiser when exhausted or sad; and a way of offering motivation and conceptualisation.

As autists struggle with communication and socialisation to varying degrees, an interest can also be a way of meeting like-minded people. It can introduce new social interactions and develop social skills, and boost the individual's confidence. Like many things, a special interest in an autistic individual can be cyclical, e.g. it can change and be replaced over time. So if parents are concerned that a child's collection is unusual, it may pass. (Or, it may develop into a thriving career, like autistic naturalist and presenter Chris Packham, who was obsessed with the natural world as a child. Chris built up many collections that others may have thought odd, like animal remains).

Another element which broadly falls under the same category as hyper-focus is obsessive thought patterns. Autists are often accused of 'not letting things go', or ruminating over something that seems inconsequential to others; this can link to obsessive compulsive tendencies. Whilst this 'stuck record' mentality may be frustrating for others, (e.g. if the autist repeatedly talks about and frets over a conversation they had, and wonders if someone was upset; or is feeling troubled by a confrontation when they felt intimidated, and continually verbalises their feelings), it's crushing for the autist. The thought process does become like a loop or stuck record, and continually plays, intruding on everything else. It can lead to impulsivity – e.g. 'having it out' with a person, making an official complaint about a service, or unnecessarily breaking ties with a friend or colleague. There's no definitive way to break this autistic pattern or cycle, although training one's brain to recognise 'stuck' patterns can help. (For someone of any neurology!)

For example –

- Recognising other accompanying stress-related signs, such as feelings of anxiety, butterflies in the tummy, higher heart rate (fitness trackers can assist here), or an increased need to stim. (See the chapter: 'S is for stimming'). If one identifies the 'stuck record' as a sign or symptom, it can be easier to look at it objectively.

- Taking a set number of deep breaths and repeating a reassuring phrase.

- Changing the environment, even if it's moving to another room. (If sensory issues are exacerbating things, a quieter or less busy area may be beneficial).

- Undertaking some exercise, even a brisk walk, or jogging on the spot, to physiologically alter one's state.

- Using some kind of sensory activity to distract the brain, maybe using pressure, like a standing press-up against a wall, or a press-up on the floor. Similarly, bouncing on a trampoline or hitting a punch bag can help with recalibration.

- Writing down the issue on paper and acknowledging that it's now 'out', and has been dealt with. (One could even create a worry post box for the letter – ideal for children).

The autist's view

I have never really experienced especially unusual interests, although I did collect many things as a child; and I obsessively loved (and still do!) a pop group that was established way before my time, that none of my friends were interested in. I have definitely experienced obsessive thought processes, whereby you have to break a 'loop' of something going around your brain repetitively; this can be very upsetting and limiting. Recognising it is key.

However, I would say to families 'struggling' with what they consider to be obsessive thought processes (and subsequent behaviours or conversation topics) that their child is experiencing that it is rarely useful to tell the autist that their issue is annoying. (E.g. 'Stop going on about it! It doesn't matter, surely?'). Sometimes with a child, it can be useful to let the 'loop' run its course, or help them with distraction techniques and mindfulness (if mindfulness works for the individual in question – not all autists find that the practice works for their neurology). In anyone (of any age or neurology), helping them work though the obsessive thought, and find a solution, can help. Identifying the issue on a traffic light system of concern (red, amber and green), or a 'cool to hot' temperature gauge of concern, may benefit the autist, in terms of self-regulation. Keeping a diary may also help, especially as a form of reflection, and to recognise that a former issue is now rectified. It's important for third parties to try to respect the individual's neurology, and accept that patterns, sameness and hyper-focus are usually key aspects of the autist's personality and make-up. And as a third party, if you can't beat 'em, join 'em; maybe it's time to learn more about the special interest too?

P is for Pathological Demand Avoidance, or PDA

PDA is widely recognised as an autistic profile – however, if it is ever featured in the media, it tends to be described as being 'a rare form of autism'. The National Autistic Society (NAS) describes PDA as being: *'Increasingly, but not universally, accepted as a behaviour profile that is seen in some individuals on the autism spectrum.'*

Key areas of concern for the autist with a PDA profile are an anxiety driven need to be in control and avoid their own and other people's demands, and an intolerance of uncertainty. As with all autists, some key difficulties experienced by individuals with PDA include social communication and interaction difficulties, as well as restrictive and repetitive processes, and some sensory challenges. The PDA Society, an organisation that provides information and support for parents, families and teachers, has some great resources on what it feels like to have PDA, and also a useful timeline of the history of PDA – see: *www.pdasociety.org.uk*. *'An individual with PDA will also have tremendous difficulty complying with their own self-imposed expectations and with doing things that they really want to do'*, advises the PDA Society. Importantly, the extreme nature and sometimes obsessive quality of the demand avoidance seen in individuals with PDA is very different to the avoidance seen in other autistic individuals. *'Specifically, people with PDA will avoid demands made by others, due to their very sudden, and usually high, anxiety levels when they feel that they are not in control,*' notes the excellent website 'The PDA Resource', which has links to various recommended websites, blogs, documents, graphics etc. (See: *www.pdaresource.com*).

But what about diagnosis? When many of the key features of PDA are present alongside the other autistic traits, individuals deemed to have PDA are still given a diagnosis of autism, however clinicians are encouraged to note that the individual has a demand avoidant profile, to help families and educators develop systems of support. One important point to note about PDA is that different clinicians and 'experts' have differing levels of experience and exposure to the profile, which is still seemingly relatively misunderstood, in a clinical sense. Meanwhile, some authorities and health bodies (in the UK at least) are reducing their autism diagnosis budgets, and a combination of factors seemingly means some clinicians are not always willing to diagnose PDA as a separate autistic profile. This author recommends the book '*Understanding Pathological Demand Avoidance Syndrome in Children: A Guide for Parents, Teachers and Other Professionals*' by Christie, Duncan, Fidler and Healy, published by Jessica Kingsley Publishers. (See: *www.tiny.cc/PChristie*). It's a great, if in depth read, and has many tips that wold work for any young autist struggling with issues surrounding uncertainty, change and avoidance of everyday tasks.

It is important to note that demand avoidance as a phrase is often taken literally by third parties, e.g. a strong request from someone to the autist to do something, e.g. wash their face, or put their shoes on. However, a demand is just something expected. It could be something 'demanding', but it could be an unspoken expectation such as wearing the shoes on the correct feet, or eating at a specific time, like lunchtime. Individuals with a PDA profile, who often describe themselves in conversation as 'PDA-ers', explain how even a desirable end result, like eating a favourite cake or visiting a fun attraction, can cause internal demand avoidance described as panic inducing, or fearful. For this reason, PDA can be very difficult to understand by outsiders, who cannot conceive how a person would resist or refuse something that they actually desire or enjoy – but the core of PDA is a neurology that seemingly causes excessive fight or flight responses for situations that do not warrant such strong feelings. Rigid environments like schools, with so many expectations and rules, are generally thought to cause PDA-ers great duress.

The NAS describes the distinctive features that someone with a demand avoidant autistic profile may have as including: resists and avoids the ordinary demands of life; uses social strategies as part of avoidance, e.g. distracting or giving excuses; appears sociable, but lacks understanding; experiences excessive mood swings and impulsivity; appears comfortable in role play and pretence; displays obsessive behaviour that is often focused on other people. The NAS explains that people with a PDA profile can appear controlling and dominating, especially when they feel anxious; however, they can also be enigmatic and charming, when they feel secure and in control (see: *www.autism.org.uk*).

The autist's view

I don't have any experience of PDA, although I did question whether a child in our family (who went onto to gain an autism diagnosis) had PDA. I found the book 'Understanding Pathological Demand Avoidance Syndrome in Children: A Guide for Parents, Teachers and Other Professionals' to be very enlightening (see: *www.tiny.cc/PChristie*). A clinical psychologist told me he wondered whether autists 'pass through' behavioural profiles such as PDA on their autistic journey, rather than specifically being born as a PDA-er, which was interesting. An element of demand avoidance is common in all autists (remember, we autists are all drawn to sameness!), but it seems unclear as to how, when or why one's neurology causes PDA to become a stand-alone profile. One community paediatrician I spoke to dismissed PDA altogether as a condition or entity, and her view isn't unusual; although her experience and exposure to complex autism presentations did seem lacking, in my opinion.

Q is for
quirks and quirkiness

Let's talk about quirks, in connection with autism spectrum neurologies. A quirk is a little difference, or something unusual – the Cambridge English Dictionary describes it as: '*An unusual habit or part of someone's personality, or something that is strange and unexpected: Or, an unusual habit, or type of behaviour.*'

Being quirky is not necessarily a bad thing; it can be a trait that makes someone fantastically individual. Lots of people are described as being quirky, and it can be a compliment; think of all the movie stars, artists and singers that you know – it is likely that the quirky ones stick in your mind the most. Lots of autistic people could be described as visually quirky. They may look quite individual – sensory challenges for example may dictate an away-from-the-norm hairstyle; meanwhile, the realisation that they don't fit into a typical mould, combined with their often boundless creativity, could influence embellishments like tattoos, fashion, hair colours and piercings. Autists are known for their sometimes-quirky special interests, which can be unusual or less mainstream than their peers' interests. Autists tend to thrive on repetition and patterns, so anything with a regular element to it appeals to the autistic brain; for example collecting certain items. The 'collection' and 'special interest' elements often intertwine, meaning autists develop real expertise in their area of interest. There is always a lot of talk (when the subject of autism arises in conversation) about the large amounts of people of all neurologies that have what could be described as autistic quirks, or traits, and this leads to the well-worn phrase: 'We're all a little bit autistic aren't we?' Put simply, no, we are not all a little bit autistic – autism is a set of cognitive differences that is diagnosed when a person matches a designated set of criteria.

What is probably meant by the above, well-worn and somewhat irritating term is that all of the population has, to a degree, traits which autistic people often also have. For example, quirks in the way one does things, repetitive habits, hyperfocus, attention to detail, shyness or introversion, and many more human traits. But to have all of the aforementioned quirks or traits does not make you autistic. It just means you have quirks in the way you do things, repetitive habits, hyperfocus, attention to detail, shyness or introversion, as examples! It is no surprise that the phrase 'We are all a little bit autistic aren't we?' gets bandied about, as it is shared from person to person – in this author's personal experience, I have heard professionals including therapists, clinicians and educators use it, when it is actually an unhelpful and confusing phrase. Thus, it is surely a matter of education. At Professor Tony Attwood's 2019 presentation, 'What you need to know about Autism', presented by the ACMAH, Professor Attwood told delegates: 'Autistic [type] characterisations are like a jigsaw of 100 pieces [e.g. 100 autistic traits] – I have never met [someone neurotypical, e.g. 'NT' or non-autistic] with less than 20 pieces, and never met someone with autism with 100.'

This author does feel however that calling quirks such as the ones listed directly below 'autistic traits' adds to the confusion. (E.g. traits linked with difficulties with social communication and social interaction, like shyness, introversion, or lacking confidence socially; restricted patterns of behaviours, e.g.

obsessive compulsive disorder-type behaviours, stimming (see the chapter: '*S is for stimming*') or tapping one's feet repetitively; and those traits linked with sensory challenges, e.g. disliking the feel of clothing labels, or avoiding a certain texture of food). In the general, NT population, these are not autistic traits, surely? Doesn't it make sense to say that only in an autist, are they autistic traits? The premise that we all have a selection of quirks, but that autists simply have more, is fine of course, but there does need to be some clarity, to get away from the '*We're all a little bit autistic aren't we?*' phrase. '*We're all a little bit quirky...*' is an improvement! Autism is widely thought to be a neurological difference in processing, and simply having a collection of traits or quirks without this difference in processing does not make someone autistic.

It is important to celebrate quirks of course, and specifically to celebrate one's autistic quirks. For a start, an autistic special interest invariably makes the individual an expert in that field – and many autistic individuals are highly creative, for example enjoying hobbies and careers in fields like photography, writing, graphic design, fashion and crafting. That 'quirk' could be the unique selling point that creates an income stream for the autist, or sets them out as a specialist, and an innovator. It could be the element that makes them the perfect friend. Another reason to celebrate quirkiness is that being different is not necessarily a bad thing. Following the crowd means you can get lost in the crowd – your voice may not be heard, you may go unnoticed, and you may coast along in the 'middle of the road'. Having a difference, a USP, means you may take unusual and creative paths. No-one changed the world by being middle of the road! (Apart from, perhaps, the Scottish pop group, Middle of the Road, who bestowed upon us the song 'Chirpy Chirpy Cheep Cheep'. The definition of how this song changed the world is perhaps up for debate!)

But back to celebrating our autistic quirks. Being different means being diverse, and diversity has shaped many key educational, economic, cultural, and societal issues. Look at the steps that have been made recently in terms of diversity of language, race, religion and gender presentation. The neurodiversity movement – described by the former conference series, the National Symposium On Neurodiversity (see: *www.tiny.cc/NSN*), as being a concept where neurological differences are to be recognised and respected, as any other human variation, and may include those individuals with Dyspraxia, Dyslexia, ADHD, Dyscalculia, Autism, Tourette Syndrome, and others – is making great strides, currently.

As described in the chapter: '*N is for neurodiversity*', the term was first used by Judy Singer, an autistic social scientist, in a publication called The Atlantic, in 1998. She saw neurodiversity as a subset of biodiversity – diversity being a 'property of populations', not individuals. Ms. Singer described her term 'neurodiversity' as: '*An umbrella movement for any 'neurotribes' who had been stigmatised for having kinds of mind-bodies that were different from the largely imaginary normal*', and by coining the phrase, explained that this was a way of '*conserving the diversity of the human species.*' Neurodiversity as a social model advocates viewing autists (and others with 'atypical cognition') as having a variation of human neurology, rather than a disease, and neurodiversity activists advocate celebrating autistic forms of communication and self-expression. Neuro-diversity advocates also promote the use of support systems that allow autistic people to live as autistic people (no need to 'cure' them or quash their autistic quirks!), and advocate simply asking autistic individuals about their experiences, to promote understanding and awareness (there's even a hashtag – *#AskAnAutistic*).

Moving onto a related subject, on the subject of quirks, it is worthwhile to look at why some NTs may see autists as being a bit too quirky, or even irritating, and examine the issue of first impressions. This section of the chapter is based on an article from *www.spectra.blog* that looked at not only interactions between autistic individuals and the people around them (of any neurology); but more importantly, how we, as autists, deal with these interactions. (Much of this content is written from this author's own perspective, so please do remember that it may not represent other autist's beliefs). The original article in question looked at the negative aspects of communication that can occur when you are autistic. A difference in neurological processing mechanisms (and therefore communication styles) is one of the key facets of being autistic, and it goes hand-in-hand with challenges in the field of socialisation.

Let's be blunt here – if you are autistic, other people of all neurologies, not just NT, may find you quirky, and even, due to a lack of understanding, irritating. It's a bitter pill to swallow when you're just being yourself. But it could be down to first impressions. As detailed further below, autists can be comparatively less expressive, or produce facial expressions that are difficult to interpret by NTs. This means others' first impressions of us can be confused, and we may appear quite quirky and even rude, or not interested in making a connection. NTs' 'programming' is described by disability rights advocate Aiyana Bailin (see: *www.tiny.cc/ABailin*) as follows: '*One of the biggest social difficulties faced by autistic people is neurotypical people's reluctance to interact with those they perceive as 'different'.*

Let's look at some autistic quirks again, in this context of two-way communication, and how others may interpret these quirks: e.g. an autist's hyper-focussed attention to detail, their focus on justice and punctuality, or a special interest that they seem over-interested in, to others. And also any quirky behaviours; e.g. an autist who stims (see the chapter: 'S is for stimming') when others see it as being inappropriate, is set out as being different, quirky or odd. Or an autist's dis-interest in social chit-chat and conventions that may make them seem distant; or an autist's differences in processing that may mean they 'lose' key words en-route from brain to mouth, or miss a conversation's meaning.

It's not ideal of course for third parties to automatically be irritated by, or distanced from autists they meet. It's not OK for autists to constantly feel belittled, or that as they can't get their interactions 'right' with people, what's the point of trying? It is not OK for NTs to roll their eyes at their autistic colleagues if they're overly pedantic about a certain issue, and it's not OK to leave the autist out of a workplace lunchtime drinks session, because the autist 'goes on about' a special, quirky interest longer than their peers may do. But it happens. And it is foolhardy not to acknowledge that these interactions and challenges happen. More than that, as an autist, knowing why people may be irritated or confused by our quirks helps us understand the process, and feel less of a failure. Communication is a two way street, and there are simply very many mixed messages and social communication differences going on at any given time.

Let's re-visit the issue of first impressions. It has been proposed that a lot of the beliefs we hold about people, and the feelings we have about them, may be made within just a tenth of a second of meeting them; the way we approach conversing with people is almost subconscious. One study by Princeton psychologists in America studied judgments from facial appearance, focusing on attractiveness, likeability, competence, trustworthiness, and aggressiveness. (See: *www.tiny.cc/1stImpression*). It concluded that there's a fraction of a second's time to make such judgements. But, autists have difficulty making appropriate facial expressions at the right times, according to a 2018 study on autistic facial expression, which used analysis of 39 studies (see: *www.tiny.cc/Trevisan*). *'[Autistics] may remain expressionless, or produce looks that are difficult to interpret,'* reported Spectrum News: (source: *www.tiny.cc/ambiguous_looks*).

Everyone essentially gets a 'feeling' about somebody upon meeting (or just observing them), and we choose to converse with them, or we choose to avoid them – this is happening in a split-second. Let's re-visit the American study on attractiveness, likeability, competence, trustworthiness, and aggressiveness. The autistic individual's lack of expression is likely to be one reason why, based on first impressions, other individuals may not get a clear impression of whether the autist is likeable.

Autists are almost universally used to being treated without respect by many people around them (again, this is not OK, but it happens); and to be blunt, we autists can annoy people – you can read about some of this author's quirks at the end of the chapter. If for example, as an autistic, you are the organised, scheduling-obsessed type (see the chapter: *'A is for Asperger Syndrome'*), like this author, other people, especially NTs, may sometimes find your hyperfocussed attention to detail and focus on aspects like truth and punctuality overwhelming. Their priorities are probably just different at that moment in time.

Conversely, if you're an autist who is sometimes challenged in the area of executive functioning skills, and for example has difficulty keeping your house as tidy as you would like, struggles with punctuality, or finds it hard to multi-task and misses what people say to you, other people may feel that you lack personal pride, or are too selfish to even get to a venue on time. They won't potentially see or understand the challenges you faced getting to the venue at all, or maybe even getting dressed, getting up that morning and stringing a coherent sentence together. They're also unlikely to consider the downsides of the interaction, and the 'social hangover' the autist may experience thereafter. See the chapter: 'H is for hangover (social)'.

It works both ways of course – if you are an autistic individual on a fast processing day, planning, scheduling, imagining and ruminating to a fast-paced soundtrack in your head, you will probably find the typical (but relatively low, when compared to yourself) processing speed of the NT people around you infuriatingly slow. You may find their sometime insistence on eye contact, interest in social hierarchy and reluctance to respect a comfortable conversational silence annoying. As an autist, you may find the sometime incessant need of NTs to chitchat and pass the time of day over trivial matters a tiring form of time stealing; especially if you are feeling sensitive and overwhelmed, due to sensory challenges. Here, it is as if one person's on slow-motion, and one person is going super-fast, from a processing point of view – and the 'slow-mo' person can seem infuriating, and their reactions and mental connections frustrating. But let's remember that many of the issues described here are simply quirks, traits and peccadillos. Everyone, of any neurology, may have quirks and habitual behaviours.

Autistic people, like many underrepresented groups, are often marginalised, belittled, ignored and even bullied. And as autists, our combined penchant for repetitive processes and our hyperfocus on certain things, which could be described by other people as 'going on about something', means another form of bullying can take place, if our quirks seem annoying or irritating.

This bulling is the belittling or disparagement of our feelings and needs, as an autist. Examples include: *'Come on, it's not that important, pull yourself together.'* *'Stop going on about it, there's other people in the world with bigger problems...'* etc. Belittling or squashing someone's emotional responses regularly just because behaviourally they are quirky can be an everyday occurrence for autists. In an ideal world, and this is something many autism advocates rightly press for, there would be widespread acceptance of people of all neurologies, as well as ethnicities, abilities and genders – we would all be accepting of each other and our quirks, we would make exceptions, we wouldn't hold grudges, we wouldn't make snap judgements, we would 'let things go', and the world would be a wonderful place whereby everyone was respectful. However, this is not currently the case, and seems unlikely to be the case, even as many individuals are being enlightened about what autism is, and how autistic individuals should be respectfully treated.

A further complication that should be noted regarding communication and acceptance of quirks is that autism runs in families, and autistic individuals are often naturally drawn to other neurodivergent individuals as friends and partners; so there is often a double element of social and communicative difficulties going on between the autist and the other individual, if the other person is autistic or neurodivergent too! E.g. they may be battling their own communication challenges, their own sense of justice, and their own quirky behaviours.

So, what can we do about this issue of mis-communication, especially if one is an undiagnosed, or a late-diagnosed autistic individual? If this describes you, you will almost certainly have spent your life feeling different – many autists describe it as being like an alien on the wrong planet – and perhaps you will have spent years constantly trying to fit in and appease people, wondering why people don't 'get' your quirks, and not really knowing why. (Masking is of course a massive and concerning issue, leading to many mental health issues for autistics, or at the very least, health concerns, because in order to fit in, many autistics camouflage their difficulties, and essentially try to appear more NT. Read more in the chapter: '*M is for masking'*). This author ponders whether we autists sometimes (even subconsciously) feel like we're actually failing to be NT; which of course can never be achieved. In this author's opinion, one of the only ways to deal with this leaning to victimhood ('*Why am I always getting it wrong? Why do my friends and family not understand me? Poor me....'*), e.g. feeling that one's feelings are being ignored, is to develop a Sod It attitude.

Yes (like all humans!), autistic people can be challenging and quirky, due to general miscommunications and preconceptions between multiple parties; and yes, other (especially NT) people often do not understand our intent; and yes, our quirks and our behaviours can lead to mistreatment. But if people are doing this on a regular basis, whether they be associates, colleagues, friends, family members, partners or whatever, maybe it would be beneficial, as an autist, to take more ownership of one's life and choices, and in the words of Keala Settle's hit song, say This Is Me. ('*I'm marching on to the beat I drum; I'm not scared to be seen, I make no apologies, this is me...'*. Lyrics from 'This Is Me', by Justin Paul / Benj Pasek).

Let's look at accepting our own quirks, as autists. As already discussed, it's our nature as autists to ruminate on things – our neurology needs repetition, and thrives on cycles; therefore, if people have treated us badly, it's common to ruminate on the situation. This cyclical issue means we can end up constantly using a negative voice about ourselves, and almost substantiating or validating the treatment that we have been given. When in fact, what would really help is to put the matter to bed, move on (not always easy for an autist!), accept that people do not necessarily understand or support our autistic selves, and focus on being the best we can be. Being ourselves, with authority; and that Sod It attitude. Most autistic individuals, as they learn more about autism themselves, endeavour to educate those around them about autism. This is partly to make their own lives easier and enlighten their friend or family member, but in general, also to spread the word and educate the wider community about the differences between NTs and autists, simply to provide understanding. That is why so many blogs and 'actually autistic' content exists, as autistic advocates strive to help develop further understanding, acceptance and awareness of autism and autistic quirks.

However, if after this stage of enlightenment, loved ones or friends are still treating you badly as an autist, citing your quirks as irritating and annoying, or not being supportive of what is important to you, or are being dismissive of your needs as an autist, is it time to break some ties? (Of course, where friends and family are concerned, this is easier said than done, and may require professional help to navigate; for example, talking therapies). But really, we do deserve better – it is surely time for autists to take ownership of our quirks, and use a Sod It attitude. We do matter, we are valid, and we do deserve respect.

The autist's view

Although you can't technically tell that someone is autistic from their outward appearance, in my experience, their quirks can be a giveaway. Autists often develop what I'd call 'autie-dar', whereby we can spot others' autistic quirks. (What enrages autists is when some parents and so-called therapists try to quash autists' quirks, to make them seem less autistic).

Something that isn't helpful to our own self-growth is when (especially as an undiagnosed autist), we don't realise that the way we do things is 'different' or challenging to some NTs. As a personal example, if I have planned something – e.g. a set of steps to achieve an end-result – I won't find it easy if someone wants to 'help' and uses a different route to the end-result. I don't like people moving my personal things (they will probably get accused of 'rummaging in my stuff'), and if I have planned a day (even if it is just in my head, and I never fully expressed it out loud), I will feel anxious if other family members want to do something else that I see as being less efficient, or change the timelines around. If I pack a suitcase, woe betide anyone that wants to re-organise it, add to it, or search for something at the bottom of the case! All of these things upset my need for sameness and control. These are just a few of my autistic quirks – now I recognise them as such, myself and my family can laugh about them and take them on board. They're often described as my 'aspie-isms', a term I don't object to. But until we all knew I was autistic, they were probably just seen as inflexible, irritating, controlling habits. I have learned that you can't fight autistic quirks, you just need to roll with them.

In terms of the elements discussed in the second half of this chapter, I believe that a sense of needing validation, or trying to appease people, is second nature to a lot of autistic people. I intrinsically avoid confrontation and generally want to please. Personally speaking, I generally try to show respect to other people, hence I feel a great sense of injustice and hurt when other people don't respect me back, or take into account my feelings. Sometimes, I know from their response that I have annoyed them, but I am not sure how. Literally by not saying a word, or by saying a word, but obviously the wrong one, I have irritated someone, when all I wanted to do was go about my day! My quirks were taken as something else, e.g. rudeness. However with research and understanding, I do now appreciate that most of what is occurring is simply mis-communication. It's a two way street (see also the chapter: '*C is for communication*'). An autism diagnosis has allowed me to recognise my own quirks, and develop something of a 'Sod it' attitude (in terms of third parties), which I am trying to cultivate further. Acceptance of our autistic quirks is what we're often searching for, as autists!

R is for
restrictive interventions

Please note, the information in this chapter relates to legal restraint used by professionals under the Mental Capacity Act 2005, using its Code of Practice. The Social Care Institute for Excellence's website (*www.scie.org.uk*) has lots of useful information, including on the Mental Capacity (Amendment) Bill, which passed into law in May 2019, and replaces the Deprivation of Liberty Safeguards.

Some autists with additional cognitive and neuro-developmental disabilities (and other co-existing conditions – see the chapter 'C *is for coexisting conditions*') may attend or live in supported facilities, attend specialist schools, or need some care within their home, to assist with every-day tasks – this means that for a proportion of their time, there could be one or more individuals looking after the autist, with responsibility for their welfare. Safeguarding can be a real issue for such autistic individuals, and recent international exposés have highlighted some dreadful cases of abuse. According to the National Autistic Society (NAS), autistic people may be at a higher risk of being abused than other people, and it can be difficult to detect that they are being abused, due to potentially limited speech, and a struggle to communicate, or identify their emotions. The organisation has lots of resources on safeguarding autists (see: *www.tiny.cc/NASsafeguarding*).

This author believes it is useful to include a mention of restrictive interventions within this book, to make readers aware of what is acceptable behaviour, from care-givers. (Restrictive interventions could include the threat of, or the use of force, as well as the restriction of an individual's movement, liberty, or freedom to act independently – e.g. restricting access or sedating them). A setting should firstly have its own intervention policies that must be adhered to, and any restrictive interventions must be necessary and proportionate – incident records should be kept. Such interventions should be used with other de-escalation techniques, e.g. trying to calm down a heightened situation, and should be a last resort; the autistic individual's care and support plan should include details of how restrictive interventions, which must meet Mental Capacity Act 2005 legislation, should be used.

Poorly applied interventions are likely to affect aspects like the autist's esteem and their quality of life, and may even cause harm – many troubling cases, some with tragic consequences, have been brought to the public's attention, recently. (A study titled *'Reducing restricted intervention of children and young people'* co-authored by The Challenging Behaviour Foundation and a Scottish support group (see: *www.challengingbehavioiur.org.uk*), found that 58% of the families questioned reported that the interventions on their child lead to injury; meanwhile, 91% reported 'emotional impacts' on the child thereafter; 78% reported that the interventions had made the original behaviours worse, while families also reported their own familial strains, breakdowns and impacts, as a result of their children's 'interventions'. The paper advised that recording and reporting of incidents must be improved.) The Royal College of Psychiatrists (see: *www.tiny.cc/RCPsych*) advises that situations where restrictive interventions may be used include: physical assault, or dangerous / threatening behaviour, e.g. by the individual to the carer in question, or another third party;

extreme over-activity by the individual that may lead to exhaustion; attempts to escape or leave a safe space; and also situations that may lead to aggression or self-harm (by the individual). Physical restraint must only be used to prevent harm to the autistic individual or others; the NAS states that almost everyone who is autistic has the ability to express a view on how they'd like to be treated, so consent for potential restraining actions should ideally be sought. NICE, the National Institute For Health And Care Excellence (see: *www.tiny.cc/N_I_C_E*), advises – *'Restrictive interventions should only be used if all attempts to diffuse the situation have failed, and the individual becomes aggressive or violent. If possible, an individual who is the same sex as the individual [that requires restraint] should carry out the restraint.'*

The autist's view

I thankfully have no personal or familial experience of the issues depicted above, but have read with alarm the various stories about restrictive interventions and abuse used against autists and other neurominorities. It is said that autists are at a higher risk of death from accidents, suicide, deaths related to self-harm, as well as epilepsy. (See: *www.tiny.cc/MortalityAutism* and *www.tiny.cc/mortality-ASD*). One can only hope that the various authorities and institutions exposed in the cases seen recently are learning from their past mistakes concerning recruitment, staff training and duty of care.

R is for rights

This UK-centric chapter looks at the legislation concerning autism – for anyone hoping to access support for themselves or their families, it is important to familiarise oneself with it.

Please note that the National Autistic Society (NAS) has extensive information at the website: *www.autism.org.uk* under the heading *'Accessing Adult Social Care – England'*, detailing how autists can access a needs assessment by social services, and what support is available.

There is legislative framework in place to protect autistic people – in the UK, this legislation includes:

* The Children Act 2004 – its main principles revolve around promoting safety and child protection. The Act covers local authorities and professionals that work with minors, and also covers the roles of parents and guardians and the UK courts, in terms of how to protect minors. This would include safeguarding (see the chapter: *'R is for restrictive interventions'*) and protecting local children, assessing their needs and promoting their upbringing by families (if safe to do so). The Act also details supervision orders, emergency protection, provision of accommodation to suitably vulnerable or abandoned minors, as well as so-called disabled children, or those with so-called special needs.

* The Children and Young person's Act 2008 – this extends the existing framework in England & Wales in terms of appropriate care for minors, and includes overseeing care placements and educational settings for 'in care' minors.

* The Education Act 2002 – this ensures that school governing bodies, local education authorities and educators have consistent arrangements to safeguard children.

* The Children and Families Act 2014 – this aims to ensure increased protection for vulnerable minors, including 'in care' children, and those with 'additional needs'. It places obligations on local authorities to produce legally binding Educational & Health Care Plans (EHCPs) for minors with such needs. EHCPs aim to make sure needs are met continually, and teachers and parents may request this. Local authorities (with health and social care commissioners) will have their own Autism Health Care Pathways, which generally include these elements (possibly with differing terminology): Local Offer (where a lead professional is selected), Team Around the Family (where an assessment need is considered, e.g. an autism assessment), Referral, and then Integrated Assessment, My Plan (including the setting's allowance of budgets), followed by My Life and My Review, e.g. goals and reviews for the individual. The aim of the process is to establish support needs, and then plan for outcomes, via a multi-agency system.

* Guidance also extends to single assessment processes, carried out by local authorities regarding welfare concerns – an assessment aims to determine if child

needs any protection, and is carried out together with the Working Together to Safeguard Children 2015 guidance. These processes are multi-disciplinary, and involve all services involved with the family.

In the UK, the National Institute for Health and Care Excellence (NICE) has guidelines for autism assessment that local authorities and health and social care commissioners should follow, in order to meet best practice, and present their own Autism Health Care Pathway (see: *www.tiny.cc/NICEpathway*). For children requiring autism assessment, Local Authorities tend to refer individuals to the Community Paediatrics team, local specialist services (depending on the need), or the Child and Adolescent Mental Health Service, or CAMHS (although this service does have 'referral thresholds' that may include 'associated mental health difficulties'). The NAS has previously criticised CAMHS (source: *www.tiny.cc/NAS_CAMHS*), stating in 2010: *'Forty four per cent of parents find it difficult to get a first referral to CAMHS for their child, with a quarter waiting over four months for a first appointment, following referral. [CAMHS] professionals told us that many of their colleagues had not had basic autism training, meaning that they could not treat mental health problems in a child with autism'.*

In the UK, there are some national statutory services available to autistic individuals and their families. For example, the Government has a duty to provide national statutory services at local level, e.g. schooling, housing, healthcare services, healthcare professionals (such as speech and language therapists), as well as child and adult services in the community, e.g. CAMHS. The Care Act 2014 and the Families Act 2014 cover assessment, care and support for those in need of it, and this legislation helps with a framework for local service providers to adhere to.

So, the above content is a brief over-view of UK legislation and statutory services. The big questions include: how easy is it to gain an autism assessment, especially for children; how is it fair that local services and waiting times differ so much across different geographical locations; is there sufficient and easy access to social care locally; and why is there (anecdotally) a seeming lack of training, understanding and awareness concerning many educators (in terms of identifying and supporting autistic pupils), and also mental health professionals? The NAS has reported that Government funding has been cut from services for disabled children and their families in England, and in 2019, joined forces with the Disabled Children's Partnership (DCP), to call on the UK Government to reinstate funding, via the DCP's 'Give it Back' campaign (see: *www.autism.org.uk*). The NAS also has extensive information at the same website under the heading *'Accessing Adult Social Care – England'*, detailing how autists can access a needs assessment by social services, and what support is available. They also detail how autistic people can access social care, services from the NHS and universal credit, as well as information on SEND school funding.

The autist's view

What has struck me on my 'autistic journey' is how much services vary across the country (UK), and one assumes, internationally. I count myself lucky to live in a county with efficient adult autism assessment, however some individuals are obviously less fortunate, and have to fight for autism assessment, or go private. The procedure for children's assessment in the UK can be frustrating. An autistic child in our family was for example referred to their local Community Paediatrics team, who performed a 'standard assessment' that included developmental, medical, social and family history, and physical examination. However they failed to carry out a complex assessment that would have included structured observations and standardised developmental interviews, completely missing the child's autism, leading to a further year's delay before the child was later assessed by (presumably) more experienced clinicians. The framework is there to gain assessment and support, but it seems that you do have to fight for it sometimes; having a familiarity with one's rights can only be beneficial.

S is for shutdown

A common question asked of someone who is autistic is: what is the difference between meltdown, shutdown and even burnout? This particular chapter will focus on autistic shutdown; and by its nature, includes content that is personal to this author. It's really important to clarify that because every autistic person is an individual, they will experience meltdown, shutdown and burnout in different ways. Shutdown, for someone who is autistic (and, in this author's opinion), can be described as feeling like a fairly old computer that's not equipped with all the modern update software – it simply has too many apps or browsers or programmes open. Autistic shutdown is when you need to start closing down your programmes to conserve energy, and generally only the most important programme (e.g. 'parenting', if you are a parent), is left on. Everything else closes down to a degree, just to conserve your own battery life – as if you keep going at your current level, you will certainly head for an autistic burnout – see the chapter: 'B is for burnout'.

Being in autistic shutdown is self-preservation mode – it is a mode that happens with your consent to a degree, as it is something that needs to happen to re-calibrate your body. Signs of shutdown (again in this author's opinion) would include one's voice getting increasingly monotone; finding it harder to make eye contact with people; your throat feeling tight when speaking; general lethargy; becoming panicky, anxious or grumpy; and finding it harder to smile and express emotion. The overriding feeling of shutdown for ·

an adult or child on the autistic spectrum is perhaps one of existing in a glass box – you are one step away from everyone, looking out of your box; if someone asks you how you are feeling, the truthful answer is probably: 'I am not.' Because your feelings are one of the programmes that have been temporarily turned off, while your body re-sets. Autistic shutdown can be spotted if you (as the autistic person) know your individual signs and triggers; or if you recognise them in your loved one. Shutdown can last any length of time; it really depends on how you are feeling and what level of self-care you are able to administer, and what challenges are currently in your life. Coming out of it might simply involve a good chat with a loved one, or removal of some external stress, some good rest, or simply some time-out; e.g. time away from external stimuli, people and interaction. Maybe some 'duvet days' in bed. Please don't underestimate the importance of recovery – if a person had a migraine, they'd probably retreat to bed to recover – and this situation is not dissimilar.

The UK's Autism West Midlands organisation (see: *www.autismwestmidlands.org.uk*) describes autistic shutdown as follows: '*During shutdown, a person may either partially or completely withdraw from the world around them. They may not respond to communication anymore, retreat to their room or lie down on the floor. They may also no longer be able to move from the situation they are in, no matter what it is (for example, a shopping centre or a classroom). Shutdowns are a person's response to reaching crisis point.*'

The autist's view

As this chapter has predominantly been this author's view, here's a comment from a person who wanted to ask me if their son, who an educational psychiatrist suggested could be autistic, may have be in shutdown. The person stated: 'My son is home from Uni, but he seems unable to function; not even basic daily tasks, finding washing and dressing very hard, taking hours to do. His thought processes are being interrupted, and he cannot think what to do next from moment to moment, like he has regressed to being a small child. He goes into frequent trances, sometimes not hearing; when he does answer, his voice is monotone.'

As I explained to the parent, based on my personal experience (and whilst not passing on any medical opinion or advice), I believe that this could describe a person who is in shutdown; they're clearly in need of recuperation. To reiterate what Autism West Midlands states: Shutdowns are a person's response to reaching crisis point. Shutdown can be very serious, and this author sees burnout (see the chapter: '*B is for burnout*') as a more drastic and long-term example of shutdown – e.g. burnout can be seen as the next, more debilitating stage, if the environment that is causing the stressors of shutdown is not changed, or addressed. Anecdotally, it seems common for autists to experience shutdown when their educational setting becomes too stressful, or too much to handle.

I have experienced shutdown on many occasions, and find that one has to become quite selfish to focus on recovering. Families of autists experiencing shutdown ideally need to help them recalibrate in a way that meets the autist's needs. As shutdowns are a response to reaching crisis point, it is usually time to rest in a low-demand environment, with as few challenges in the areas of communication, sensory triggers and socialisation as is possible. It could be as simple as having one or two quiet days like this, to help the autist recalibrate! Talking therapies may help with longer-term issues.

S is for stimming

Understanding stims is key to understanding how autists process emotions and sensory input. Stims, and the action of stimming, refers to 'self-stimulating' behaviours; they're not limited to autists (many people twirl their hair, or tap their fingers to an imaginary beat, for example); but most autists stim. Stims may be used for various reasons; for example in times of anxiety; in periods of happiness or contentment; when the body is in need of regulation; and simply because the individual feels good. Most people, if they have heard of autism stims, think of hand flapping, which is the stereotypical one used most commonly in connection with fictional autistic characters. But perhaps rightly so, as a repetitive hand movement is a very common stim, in terms of dis-regulation, sensory overload or anxiety. Most autistic individuals stim to some degree; they can be very subtle however, and autists who are late-diagnosed may not even realise that their habitual behaviours are stims. For example, clasping or rubbing one's hands together, or wrapping hair around a finger. Here are some examples of autistic stimming –

* Clapping or flapping the hands, or moving them rhythmically.

* Finger clicking or snapping, e.g. with the thumb and third finger.

* Beating out a rhythm with the hands or fingers (and feet), to a beat in your head.

* Flicking or stroking fingernails.

* Playing with jewellery, especially if it has movement, e.g. a ring with a spinning section.

* Touching something smoothly tactile, like a watch, a clothing label, or piece of jewellery.

* Proprioceptive stims, e.g. rocking or moving the body – and as well as a 'big' movement, this can be the tiniest movement, for example isolating and clenching a small muscle. Proprioceptive stims can also include pressure stims, perhaps sitting in a certain way to achieve a sense of pressure; or moving the joints to achieve a 'click', or mobilisation – e.g. moving the joint to the edge of its socket.

* Vocal stims – e.g. humming; singing without recognisable words; and making mouth noises (for example sucking on the teeth or cheeks, or clicking the tongue).

* Cognitive stims – these seemingly provide some kind of sense of control or regularity; examples include performing a particular numerical sum, or counting in a particular formation.

* Echolalia – in this context, a favoured phrase or number sequence that sounds appealing may be used as a stim. (See the chapter: 'E is for echolalia').

* Other stims – there are further stims that an autist may carry out, such as: visual stimming, e.g. staring at lights or an interesting kinetic picture, or watching a spinning object; auditory stims, e.g. listening to the same song on a loop; olfactory and oral stims, such as

sniffing objects or licking and chewing on things; and facial tics and features of Tourette Syndrome.

* Self-injurious stims – some individuals may direct a repetitive action on themselves, e.g. hitting their head or face, or may carry out dermatillomania (picking at the skin, e.g. scabs or hairs), or trichotillomania (hair plucking). Stims like this can be detrimental; e.g. in the case of hitting oneself, they are not desirable or helpful in the long term, and can lead to self-harm. In such cases the need to stim may be directed to another object, such as a squeezy toy or boxing punchbag. Using pressure or movement may also be a useful alternative to injurious stims, e.g. pressing the hands against a wall, pressing up from the floor, or bouncing on a Swiss ball. Weighted pressure blankets may also be useful, e.g. to sit or lie under. These 'tools' may work to help redress sensory dis-regulation, if this is the cause of the stim.

Although some proponents of coercive behavioural 'therapy' aimed at autists seemingly seek to reduce stims, and frame them as some kind of antisocial behaviour, in fact there is nothing wrong with non-injurious autistic stims. Remember that autistic individuals may have problems not only with processing feelings, but also sharing their emotions in the expected way. Stims are very often a way of putting an emotion into a physical representation. The above everyday examples of behavioural stims are perfectly normal and acceptable, especially in children who are finding a place in the world; non-injurious stims should not be discouraged. They are simply a way of recalibrating, finding a sense of calm, and satisfying an inbuilt need for repetition. *'Autistics are easily overloaded, and simply need to release tension more frequently. When I stim, I often feel like an old fashioned boiler letting off pressure; sometimes in tiny bursts, sometimes in huge belches of steam,'* writes Kirsten Lindsmith. (Source: *www.tiny.cc/KLindsmith*). Stims can represent valuable communicative information, if an autist finds (in that moment) talking difficult. A stim can indicate rising anxiety, for example. This is valuable information for family members accompanying a young autistic child somewhere, and a potential sign that the environment could be stressful.

In situations such as the workplace, where autistic stims are not necessarily encouraged or accepted, there are ways to make them less noticeable; e.g. there are many fidget toys or gadgets like pens, chewy stim toys and pieces of tactile jewellery that can divert attention.

Many autistic women for example enjoy having smooth, manicured nails that fulfil a nice sensory need, and touching the nails can be very discreet. Sensory challenges are often cited as big causative factors for stims, as the stimming can create a tactile input (e.g. flicking a muslin or blanket, or a clothes label). The action can help self-soothe and calm the individual, if the stim is linked to anxiety or over / under stimulation from noise, lights, socialisation etc. Some autists believe that stimming can actually cause the release of beta-endorphins in the body, which then causes a feeling of 'numbness' from sensory overload, or plain old pleasure.

The autist's view

The main reason autists stim seem to be to block out excess sensory input, manage emotions, provide extra sensory input, reduce discomfort, or self-regulate. Personally speaking, I am not a big 'stimmer' – however I do frequently stroke one of my thumbnails with that forefinger, and like to keep it smooth for this reason. A rough-feeling nail varnish, e.g. something glittery, would feel quite abhorrent to me! I do it when I am feeling self-conscious or apprehensive (at these times, I may dig the thumb nail into my finger, to provide a sort of distraction), but also just when I am relaxed, as a parent would stroke a child's head, to give comfort. I like smooth jewellery and precious stones, and will often touch a nice-feeling necklace pendant, or twiddle it, just as a self-regulatory act. (At school, I had a terrible proprioceptive stim, when I used to 'click' one hip joint to the edge of its socket. It has left that joint comparatively weak, as an adult.)

S is for spoons theory

This chapter contains information on the popular disability metaphor, the spoons theory. It is partly replicated in the chapter: '*H is for hangover (social)*'. All autists use many, many 'spoons' or energy units when they socialise, experience sensory input and go about their daily business. Not heard of the spoons theory? It was developed quite by chance by Christine Miserandino, who has lupus, and uses 'spoons' to explain how to ration one's energy. The spoons theory maintains that a person with a reduction in energy levels (emotional or physical), starts the day with a certain number of spoons. Each spoon represents a burst of energy; so showering, getting dressed etc requires small numbers of spoons, as does conversing with close friends and family at home. Some activities, for example, meeting a group of friends or colleagues, being interviewed, chatting in a public place, require lots of spoons. Therefore, autists often find that, due to their autistic challenges – e.g. social communication and social interaction issues, as well as sensory challenges – great chunks of their energy may be used up more quickly than that of their neurotypical (NT) peers and family members.

Let's take an average day for a busy working autist Mum; let's say she has 12 spoons of (mainly emotional) energy that day, which was Christine Miserandino's original proposition.

Get up and complete the morning duties and the school run. Two spoons.

Do a few hours at her part time job. Four spoons.

Do the school run and complete the afternoon family duties. Two spoons.

Cook tea and manage the child's bedtime regime. Two spoons.

Converse with her family. Two spoons.

That's all her energy used up.

But what if something unexpected happens – e.g. a phone call from a relative that was emotionally draining; a long chat at the school gates with a fellow parent; an impromptu talk with the teacher; or a neighbour wanting to chat? These require spoons, and our theoretical autist Mum has none left. In an ideal world, she would realise her spoon allocation had 'run over' that day, and would plan for a quieter day the next day, to recalibrate. Maybe using self-care tools like headphone-time listening to music, reading a book, having a nap, or whatever works for her. But what if our Mum wanted to arrange some social time with a friend or family? Dinner perhaps, a little shopping spree, time at the park with the kids, a trip to a local attraction? It's likely this would use up a massive part of her daily spoon allowance. (Especially as there's very likely to be background music, extra lighting, or noisy chatter thrown into the sensory melting pot). So, she'd have to plan for both a low-spoon day on the day of the social visit, and probably the next day too, to recalibrate. If her spoon-management wasn't up to speed, our autist would likely suffer from a 'social hangover' – see the chapter: 'H is for hangover (social)'.

Writing on the Sydney Morning Herald (*www.tiny.cc/ spoonstheory*), Naomi Chainey writes; '*Spoons are for essentials. The remainder of the day is for bedrest. Any more activity will result in less spoons tomorrow. When life presents unexpected tasks that can't wait, my spoons get rearranged. My daily quota doesn't always match my plans.'* (Incidentally, thanks to the spoons theory, many people with invisible illnesses refer to themselves as 'spoonies' – there are even hashtags like #Spoonie and #SpoonieChat, to aid online discussions!)

The autist's view

I love the spoons theory. There are other metaphors – like the cup that runneth over, the bucket that overflows, or the device that's used up its bandwidth – but the spoons theory is so simple and organic. I also love Naomi Chainey's description that: 'When life presents unexpected tasks that can't wait, my spoons get rearranged. My daily quota doesn't always match my plans.' For an autistic person, this describes the situation perfectly. We can all make plans to the best of our abilities, but life presents unexpected incidences constantly. Personally, I am an over-scheduler. I love to arrange, book, plan and schedule things – it suits my need for control and organisation. However I am prone to over-booking, forgetting that simple, everyday things like going shopping, doing the school run and 'mumming' also all require spoons. However I am trying to be kinder to myself and allow some down-time – this undoubtedly helps 'replenish' the spoons!

T is for toxins

While there's no specific known cause for autism, much work has been done within the genealogy field, leaving many experts to cite *'interactions between susceptible genes and environmental factors'* as likely causative factors. E.g. autism is known to run in families, with certain genes associated with it – but some experts believe that so-called environmental (or non-genetic) factors (for example, the mother's health status in pregnancy, the use of some medicines, and her exposure to certain compounds); may 'turn on' susceptible genes, or somehow increase their risk factors for neurologies like autism. (See: *www.tiny.cc/PKarimi*).

In the author's opinion, there is currently no sound evidence pointing to any causative links between vaccines and autism. The NHS widely states that: *'No link between the MMR vaccine and autism'* has been found – (see: *www.tiny.cc/MMRautism*). In the NHS Public Health England document, *'NHS public health functions agreement 2018-19, Service specification No.10, Measles, mumps and rubella (MMR) immunisation programme'*, experts advise that as a direct result of scaremongering about vaccinations: *'The rise in measles cases seen in 2013 can be mostly attributed to the proportion of unprotected 10-16 year olds who missed out on vaccination in the late 1990s and early 2000s, when concern around the discredited link between the vaccine and autism was widespread.'* (Source: *www.tiny.cc/MMautism2*). Scandalously, the UK had, at the time of writing this book, lost its official measles-free country status from the World Health Organisation after a gradual fall in rates of MMR (measles, mumps and rubella) immunisation. British politicians are currently encouraging parents to ignore the 'fake news' about autism and vaccines, and British leaders are calling for social media companies to discuss how they can play their part in promoting accurate information about vaccinations, moving forward.

There are some links between autism and environmental factors, e.g. toxins. One study examined baby teeth from autistic children, and correlated the metals lead, zinc and manganese (source: *www.tiny.cc/TeethHeavyMetals*). Published in the journal Nature Communications, the (small) study found that baby teeth from autistic children contained more toxic lead, and less of the essential nutrients zinc and manganese, compared to teeth from non-autistic children. Whilst proposing that autism likely 'begins' in the womb, researchers proposed that 'environment' can increase a child's risk of being born autistic. (Of course, studies can have different interpretations, according to the experiences, values and beliefs of the people reading them). There are also studies linking the pregnant mother's immune response, e.g. 'abnormal maternal immune activation', and the resulting, elevated levels of inflammatory cytokines, which are said to affect the baby's embryonic brain development, and increase the risk of autism. (Source: *www.tiny.cc/PKarimi*). This particular study states – '*Mother exposure to some chemicals [including] heavy metals... can affect foetal health negatively through epigenetic alterations of gene expression.*' Our bodies produce 'adrenal steroids' or stress hormones such as cortisol, and there are also theories relating to 'placental permeability' to these hormones, when the mother is pregnant. Heavy metals are of course a much-discussed issue in connection to autism. A recent and very contentious study linked overloads of aluminium to autism (although this was a very small study of five individuals, and in some detractors' opinions, didn't use suitable controls, so was not very 'robust'). Readers may like to see the article: 'Using bad science to demonize aluminum adjuvants in vaccines', which delves into more detail, challenges the contentious study itself, and contains links to further information (see: www.tiny.cc/adjuvants).

But why are so many individuals being so fanatical about causative factors for autism? There's certainly lots of research underway searching for these causative factors. Let's consider why this could be – the 'Neurodivergent Collective', writing at the website: www.theaspergian.com states that one factor could be that the so-called 'genetics/cure lobby' are recipients of a substantial percentage of the trillions of dollars spent internationally on autism. 'This includes pharmaceutical companies, genetics researchers, corporate lobbyists, and investors,' the website prudently suggests. (Please do read their excellent article at: www.tiny.cc/aspergian – it raises some very interesting points, and utilises the hashtag #AltAutism.)

In this author's opinion, families of autists would perhaps be better served supporting their autistic family member by helping them manage their autistic challenges via aspects like talking therapies, the reduction of 'demands' (to help reduce anxiety) etc, rather than embarking on non-proven, 'quack' ways to help reduce so-called autistic symptoms (or god forbid, 'cure' autism). This author believes that independent scientists (not tied to pharmaceutical companies) and psychologists should of course be left to research and present their theories on autism; but that the rest of us are perhaps better off promoting empathetic autism awareness – not seeking causes and 'cures'. (Now is a good time to reiterate that autism is widely regarded as a difference in processing and is not a disease.) In this author's experience of research, and of participating in social media groups, there is clearly a big movement consisting of parents of young autists who are focusing extensively on the issue of toxins, (e.g. heavy metal overload, as well as vaccines), and their impact on autistic individuals. But in the course of this author's work at *www.spectra.blog*, extensively reading and researching articles and papers, the author has seen no irrefutable evidence in the field of heavy metals and autism, in terms of the toxins being a definitive causative factor. Yes, there are studies linking environmental factors to autism that investigate how certain compounds may 'turn on' susceptible genes, or somehow increase risk factors for autism. But these studies should not lead parents and families to take action by furtively administering potions to their children in the hopes of 'curing' them, in this author's opinion. There are reportedly some horrifying, abusive practices going on the world over, whereby families of autists administer chemicals to their children orally, through enemas, or in baths, which are supposedly thought to 'cure' autism. This field of research (into environmental toxins) is still relatively young, so we do need independent, robust studies and facts, to help us make informed decisions – and these independent, robust studies are seemingly hard to come by. The recent contentious piece of research on aluminium (see the article at *www.tiny.cc/adjuvants*) for example looked at five (decreased) autistic subjects. Detractors of the study ponder whether, for such concepts to be taken seriously, studies like these (that may lead to individuals giving their autistic family members oral compounds to help 'cure' their autism, or reduce the 'traits') should be more robust. This author advises that interested parties researching such matters should always check who funded a study, and consider what gains the funding organisation may reap, when searching for information relating to environmental toxins and autism.

On the subject of studies, one article (see: *www.tiny.cc/C-sect*) reported on a very credible study (see: *www.tiny.cc/C-sect2*) that found higher rates of caesarean section (CS) deliveries in autistic children. The study stated: '*This study confirms previous findings that children born by CS are approximately 20% more likely to be diagnosed as having ASD (autism spectrum disorder)*'. Many people reviewing and discussing the article and study results thereafter asked whether C-sections were a causative factor for autism – however, this author's viewpoint is instead to question why the autistic babies did not deliver naturally? This author would therefore urge anyone interested in reading more about autism and the effects of so-called toxins to 'delve deep' into the research, and remember that studies can have different inter-pretations, according to the experiences and beliefs of the people reading them.

One thing which is interesting is that inflammation is widely cred-ited with being linked to autism; that seems consistent. And yes, environmental factors do potentially seem to be linked to the onset of autism, in terms of how a developing baby's body processes compounds in the womb (source: *www.tiny.cc/PKarimi*). With sci-ence advancing, there is the possibility that new studies will come out that do conclusively and specifically link toxins to autism; but this author's belief is that some of the current studies are simply not convincing or robust enough. (In this author's opinion, there are far better things for people interested in learning more about autism to read and learn about, than 'detoxing' children (usually without their consent) from toxins; for example, SEND support in schools, the male / female divide in autism, and the process of re-ferral and diagnosis for autistic children in the local authority system. Have some people got their priorities skewed?)

As mentioned, in this author's experience of reading about and researching autism, inflammation certainly seems to be a factor with many autistic individuals, as are digestive challenges. The causes are seemingly unknown, but some individuals propose that stress hormones could be a factor. While this author would never engage in harmful practices like using oral compounds to detox from 'toxic overload' to reduce so-called autistic symptoms, I am open to the concept of supporting an autistic individual's body through a healthy diet, and managing their stress levels, so that physical signs of stress may be reduced. (Please remember, the UK's National Health Service advises: 'There are no treatments or cures for autism itself. Special diets – such as gluten-free, casein-free or ketogenic - can be harmful.)

The autist's view

I am interested to read articles and studies citing the fact that inflammation seems to be a factor with many autistic individuals, as well as digestive challenges. The causes are seemingly unknown, but some individuals propose that stress hormones could be a factor. While this author would never engage in harmful practices like using oral compounds to detox from 'toxic overload' to reduce so-called autistic symptoms, I am open to the concept of supporting an autistic individual's body through a healthy diet, and managing their stress levels, so that physical signs of stress may be reduced.

U is for understanding the autism filter

It is sometimes tempting for third parties to think of autism like a face-mask or pair of glasses that an autistic individual puts on – as if their true self is beneath, and the face-mask or glasses sit atop. But this would mean that the accessories (or their autism) can be cast away, which isn't the case. If modern theories are correct, an autist's autism was there since they developed in utero, and will be there until they die. For an autistic child, when we see behaviour that challenges – such as impulsivity, irrationality and demand avoidance – it's tempting to see all of these behaviours as choices. As if the child were able to add or remove their 'autisticness', and their 'true self' made the poor decisions. On days when the individual appears 'less autistic' – e.g. more relaxed, aware of the effect of their behaviours, and less panicked about making choices – it may seem as if this is the real individual, and that autism is their alter-ego or shadow. Or that autism over-shadows them.

But in reality, what is happening is likely to be that on their 'appearing less autistic' days, the autist is less stressed and anxious; feeling more in control; has more certainty in their day; and is exercising skill-sets that mean their capability to cope with life meets or exceeds their challenges. Likewise, on their 'more autistic days', the challenges facing them – socially, emotionally and from a sensory perspective – are likely to be exceeding their emotional toolkit, and 'life skill-sets'. Therefore, could we say that autism can be seen as a filter or a frame through which our brain (that of an autistic individual), processes, sees and experiences the world around us? It is never separate from the 'real' us. It is the real us.

This way of thinking – e.g. the autism filter – may help us understand some so-called challenging behaviour exhibited by an autistic child. The question should ideally be (from family members or educators); what's missing from their skill-sets? What's causing their panic or confusion; what 'outside' demands could be reduced? And what self-care is needed to allow their brain to recalibrate and become 'unstuck'? Sometimes the answer is skewed, in that what seems appealing to an NT (neurotypical) mind causes conflict for an autist. For example: the sumptuous multiple choice breakfast buffet on holiday that's too confusing; the funfair that stimulates too many senses; the birthday event that is populated by too many guests, even if they're known and loved. In an education setting, a favourite book may become an emotional barrier if the reading space is too noisy or busy; an eager and able mind may decide something is 'too hard' if too many people are watching; the apprehension about a photo being taken after an event may cause anxiety about the event itself; and the fear of failure, or of not meeting one's own impossibly high standards, may mean a project isn't completed, even if it involves a favourite character or subject. This invisible 'cause' of unfathomable behaviour is the autism filter.

Life with a young autist, or as a young autist, will always be a balancing act between challenges and coping mechanisms. Educators and parents need to become canny problem solvers and lateral thinkers, in order to spot the root cause of a frustrating or non-sensical (seeming) behaviour. Then, sometimes the puzzle is unlocked. (But trying to work out an autist's train of thought as if they were an NT can often get in the way of finding the answers!)

The autist's view

As described, many third parties perhaps consider autism to be like a hat or pair of glasses that an autistic individual puts on – as if their true self is beneath, and the hat or glasses are placed on top. In this line of thinking, the person is With Autism; it is an addition to their true selves. There's a phrase used by some so-called autism-martyr parents along the lines of: 'We love our children, but we do not love the autism', which supports this school of thought. However, I would say that this is not a helpful thought process; it leads to anger at 'the autism', as if it has 'taken away' the child (or individual of any age), or an aspect of them. If a child some days appears to be 'less autistic', it is likely that their skill-sets exceed their challenges that day, and that their anxieties are low. It is not that this is their 'true self' – as if their true self were a more pleasant version, and the autism 'hat' is put on some days, covering the 'real' person's personality.

Let me share a story. Post-diagnosis, I had a terrifying (and informative) nightmare, whereby I was in an eerie, unknown room, and a female mannequin came to life and we began physically fighting. I had been experiencing quite violent dreams regularly, in recent weeks. Once I woke up, I was able to work out that the mannequin represented autism, and that there was no point in fighting it. (The dreams stopped thereafter). I would say to parents and family members of autists, you can't fight autism – your own ideas about common sense, e.g. what makes sense in that moment as a conclusion or consequence, don't always 'fit' with autism's sensibilities. It is usually about developing an autist's skill-sets, life-experience and coping mechanisms. Autism will always be there, as the filter through which the autist sees and experiences the world.

V is for visualising autism

Within this chapter is some information that may help us look at the autism filter in more detail, and consider the autist's 'outlook'; it is taken from one of the articles published at: *www.spectra.blog*, and is a personal musing. In this author's experience, far too many clinicians and family members are confused about what autism is, and what autism looks like. Autism is a configuration of neurology. If a person was a tree, could we visualise their autism as the trunk of the tree? Autism runs through the tree like a stick of rock, and it was there from the first time the roots began to grow. The big branches could be significant co-existing conditions, such as intellectual disabilities, Fragile-X Syndrome, epilepsy and other serious conditions. The smaller branches could be co-existing conditions such as mental health challenges, anxiety, sensory processing disorders, Attention Deficit Hyperactivity Disorder (ADHD), Obsessive Compulsive Disorder (OCD), etc. (See also the chapter: *'C is for co-existing conditions'*). The foliage is the individual autist's personality and traits, and their ability to 'mask', or blend into a neurotypical world (see the chapter: *'M is for masking'*).

Why use this analogy? Because dated autism terms like 'high functioning autism' confuse the issue – hence, it's not uncommon to come across individuals saying unhelpful things of autistic individuals, such as: *'He/she doesn't look autistic; or act autistic'*. (See the chapter: *'L is for labels and language'*.)

This is because, an autist without certain cognitive / developmental disabilities, e.g. someone who could be said to be a 'high functioning' autistic, may sometimes appear to be neurotypical (NT); but autism is there, running through their core. If we consider autism using the tree analogy, it answers the question of why autism cannot always be seen; e.g. when a family member queries that their relative could be autistic, or when a teacher can't see any issues; because the 'foliage' is masking the child's feelings and emotions.

The autist's view

I like my 'tree analogy', and hope it helps others to understand the concept that autism was always present from when the roots were first laid down, and runs through an autist's centre. The view from the outside is usually the foliage – the outer presentation. I would reiterate that autism can be considered a filter or a frame through which an autist's brain, processes, sees and experiences the world. It is never separate from the 'real' us. It is the real us.

W is for Wing (Lorna Wing)

Dr Lorna Wing was one of the most influential individuals in the field of autism. She coined the term Asperger's, and was a co-founder of the National Autistic Society. A respected psychiatrist and mother to an autistic daughter, Lorna launched a landmark study of autism in the late 1970s, with Dr Judith Gould. This led to the oft-quoted figure of one in 100 individuals being autistic, placing the condition as a more common neurology than was previously thought. Wing and Gould also developed the Diagnostic Interview for Social and Communication Disorders (DISCO), which is still widely used diagnostically. In 1981, Lorna Wing coined the term Asperger Syndrome (see the chapter: *'A is for Asperger Syndrome'*), obviously being unaware, as everyone else at the time also was, of the man's Nazi links.

She told the UK's Guardian newspaper in 2011. *'I do believe you need autistic traits for real success in science and the arts, and I am fascinated by the behaviours and personalities of musicians and scientists.'*

Her legacy lives on. The National Autistic Society's Lorna Wing Centre for Autism in Kent was one of the first centres in the country to provide diagnostic, assessment and advice service for children, adolescents and adults with social and communication disorders throughout the UK. According to the NAS, originally known as the Centre for Social and Communication Disorders, it was founded by Judith Gould and Lorna Wing under the auspices of the National Autistic Society in 1991, and was set up because parents of children suspected to be autistic, as well as other related conditions, often had major problems accessing a diagnostic assessment or an explanation for their child's behaviour. There is also a Lorna Wing Centre for Autism in Essex, again run under the auspices of the NAS.

Her contribution to autism understanding and research cannot be underestimated, and many autists owe a great deal to her determination to support autistic children whose needs were not being met in society.

The autist's view

There are very many resources on Lorna Wing – in particular, the British national newspapers ran extensive obituaries about her, which are available online with an internet search. The British Medical Journal's full page obituary on Ms. Wing is very comprehensive (see: *www.tiny.cc/LornaWING*). For further information on the early years of autism's history, including Dr. Asperger's contributions, and those of Lorna Wing, I recommend reading American writer and autism expert Steve Silberman's book, 'Neurotribes'; a very well-written piece of autism back-history. (Visit: *www.tiny.cc/Neurotribes*).

X is for expressive and receptive language

Expressive language is the use of words, sentences, gestures and writing, to convey meaning and messages to others. Receptive language is the ability to understand information, including the meaning of what others say, or what is read. The Australian website Kid Sense (*www.childdevelopment.com.au*) describes expressive language skills as including being able to label objects in the environment, describe actions and events, put words together in sentences, and use grammar correctly (e.g. '*I had a drink*' instead of '*Me drinked*'), retell a story, answer questions, and write a story.

Expertise in verbal expressive language can be limited, in autists. Or, it may be delayed – the child may 'catch up' with their peers in due course. In order to convey meaning and message, one needs many things, including good attention and concentration, pre-language skills like gestures, facial expressions and eye contact, and the motivation to communicate with others. Autists generally struggle in these areas. Autistic children are often said to show impairments in both the comprehension and the production of language, in varying degrees. The teaching resource 'Autism Classroom' states: '*Students with ASD have difficulty knowing how to use language effectively to get basic needs or social needs met.*' (Source: *www.tiny.cc/eXpressive*). In children, difficulties with language can be early signs of autism. E.g. excessive pointing or gesturing to get a message across, instead of speaking; a lack of variation in intonation or volume when the child does speak (monotone voice); differences in the use of social language, when compared to peers; and a general lack of 'to and fro' conversation with third parties. The difficulties with the flow, or 'to and fro' of conversation, can often be seen as difficulties describing, defining, explaining, and retelling events. (This goes further than the standard *'I don't know' answer* to the question, *'What did you do at school today?'*) Remember, autists have difficulties with communication from a social perspective – it isn't necessarily important to them to gain validation from peers, or share experiences for sharing's sake!

It has to be said (as one of the core facets of autism is difficulties in communication) that receptive language can also be a big issue for autists. As discussed, receptive language is the ability to understand information, including the meaning of what others say, or what is read. Sometimes though, it isn't simply an inability to understand information; it's a delay in processing it. (Autism is, after all, widely thought to be intrinsically a processing difference.) 'Getting' the meaning of what others say is probably one of the biggest challenges for autists, in terms of receptive language; especially social banter, inference and sarcasm. Expressive language is the second part of the communicative chain, and goes on to put these 'receptive' concepts described directly above into words and sentences, in a way that makes sense, and is grammatically accurate. (Many studies show that autistic children's receptive ability can be more impaired than their expressive ability (see: *www.tiny.cc/ReceptiveLanguage*).

However, language skills can be developed, and vocabulary can be built. There are also various ways for non-speakers (or those who are currently pre-verbal) to communicate. The teaching resource 'Autism Classroom' is one of many to advocate the

Picture Exchange Communication System (PECS), a tool for non-speaking individuals, that teaches the process of communication with an emphasis on initiation – starting the communicative process off. (We should take a moment within this chapter to remember that speech and communication differences are not necessarily indicators of intellectual ability. *'Communication is a complex cognitive and motor activity... [skills are] developmental and have a number of components. Communication includes semantics (understanding the meaning of words) and pragmatics (social use) of language'*, explains a study titled *'Language disorders and Autism'*; source: *www.tiny.cc/WRAY*). So, even though an autist may lack the motor activity for speech, and / or the understanding of some vocabulary meanings; may have a poor attention or concentration span; could experience difficulties reading facial and body language gestures; and may lack the motivation to develop communication skills with others; it does not mean they have low intellect!)

On the subject of what a third party views as an autist's level of understanding, the author will take a moment here to add that many autists find verbalising their understanding of language and conversation difficult; but not necessarily comprehending it. As the author describes below, an autist may well under-stand the information or conversation, or what they have read (e.g. receptive language); and may well be adept at utilising words and sentences to convey meaning and messages to others (e.g. expressive language); but in their heads, rather than via verbalisation! Sometimes on the journey from brain to mouth, this comprehension loses momentum.

So, how can expressive and receptive language skills be improved? Most of the resources are aimed at children. The 'Autism Classroom' site advocates that: *'Scripts [and adapted books] are a terrific way to help students initiate delivering messages and a variety of other types of communication. They are a great way to expand language to go beyond requesting, to commenting and conversation,'* the website explains. Depending on an autistic child's abilities, a speech and language therapist may be able to assist with difficulties with language; classroom instructions/interventions in a school setting that utilise visual or multi-media supports (e.g. pictures or videos) that initiate conversation can also be useful.

The resource 'Autism Spectrum Australia' has created a useful document entitled *'Developing Expressive Language Skills'* (*www.tiny.cc/EXPRESSIVE*). It is a great tool for educators, and includes gems such as: *'Song and rhythm is a powerful teaching tool for students with an ASD, who seem to retain the lyrics of songs far more efficiently than they would ordinary speech.'* Their document *'Strategies to develop receptive language'* is also useful, (see: *www.tiny.cc/RECEPTIVE*), and includes tips like using (with autistic children), explicit, concise and concrete language (with key words), without excessive information that may overload the child's processing capabilities. The document also suggests trying to obtain the child's attention before giving an instruction, e.g. by addressing the student by his/her name.

There is a great variety of visual supports available to help autists improve communication and language, e.g. games using photos, symbols etc. Visual supports (which include PECS), are widely considered to be one of the most effective supports for autists with communication difficulties. See also the chapter: *'C is for communication'*, which includes information on verbal and non-verbal communication.

The autist's view

There are so many issues of communication that autists struggle with, from taking things literally, to missing intonations of speech; as well as physical issues, like apraxia of speech, when speech movement (coordinated via the brain, to the lips, jaw and tongue) is difficult or impossible. What I would say is that in my experience, what many autists find difficult concerning language is verbalising it, not comprehending it. For example, an autist may well understand the information, or what they have read (receptive); and may well be adept at utilising words and sentences to convey meaning and messages to others (expressive); but more so in writing, or in their heads! Verbalising their understanding socially can be trickier. It is important for families and educators to recognise this, and not dismiss someone's understanding just because the conveyance of the understanding was not delivered in the expected way! As an example, on many times during important conversations (and heated discussions), I find that I can't say what I want to – I can't put into words what is very clear in my mind. I dare say this is related to over-whelm. Sometimes, the right words pop up a little later, when one's head has re-calibrated or calmed down.

I would say that sign language (whether British sign language, American sign language or Makaton, or the family's own made-up signs) can be useful for young autists – not simply if they're non-speakers, but also to use on days when they're emotionally tired or overwhelmed. (I wrote a book for babies and young children called 'Alfie's Magic Hat: Fun At The Zoo', which utilises these signing methods, and is widely available online.) If one has a child who struggles with expressive and receptive language, it is good to know that verbal language skills can be developed; but the learning and development will likely take place at the young autist's own pace, organically. Once one has got one's head around how the autistic mind works, it is much easier to tailor games and educational interventions aimed at improving language and communication for a child.

Y is for your family

This chapter sources an article aimed at friends and family members of autists, published on the *www.spectra.blog* website, that explores the subsequent relationships and conversations one might have, post autism diagnosis. It is written from the author's perspective.

I get asked all the time how it feels to be autistic – my friends and family are all super interested to get some kind of perspective, and see things from my point of view. That's not true. Of course it's not. They couldn't give a monkey's. It would probably be like me asking my left-handed / tall / visually-impaired / frightfully-clever friends how it feels to be them, or how it affects their day to day life. Once the fact that they're left-handed / tall / visually-impaired / frightfully-clever has been established, there's probably no conversational need to re-visit it. *"So, with you being so tall an' all, how did you feel when that really tall politician got into office?"* I can see how that line of conversation would be surplus to requirements. But some-how, one's autism does seem to warrant more discussion. If I can elaborate, I think what friends and family are theorising, once their loved one has disclosed their autism diagnosis, is that there's now a reason why the loved one is quirky / likes their own space / ran out of the driving examiner's office that time / doesn't like their fish and chips touching, etc. A nice, tidy label that explains things, but doesn't warrant further investigation. Like being told you have unmanageable hair and a double crown. This is rarely true however. We're likely to be talking about adults here (in the context of someone telling a friend/family member about their autism diagnosis), and an autistic adult who's gained a diagnosis later in life will have been greatly affected by the simple fact they're autistic. (While we tend to avoid phrases like disorder in general parlance, autism can of course make one feel dis-ordered / less ordered / requiring order.)

So, can the author implore friends and families of recently diagnosed autists not to 'package up' and hide away conversations about how the loved one's autism is affecting them? Essentially, if one is autistic, it is (and has always been) a filter through which their life is viewed. A pair of glasses, or a window frame if you will, through which we (autists) see and process everything. That work decision we made? It was made through an autism lens. The new jacket we bought? Selected through an autism lens. That big social family gathering we endured that left us exhausted, with a social hangover? (See the chapter: 'H is for hangover (social).' Yes, it was endured through an autism lens. And the filtering and processing of past events; deaths, births, marriages, work-events, friendships, fall-outs, you name it – all tackled with this different, sometimes other-worldly filter in place.

A new autism diagnosis isn't just a plaster or band aid that sticks together a few health issues. For example, someone may share with their family that the health issue they were experiencing was a result of a mineral deficiency – and a diagnosis and a supplement rectifies it. Or maybe they couldn't perform a particular physical movement because of an old injury – and a diagnosis and physio session rectifies it. An autism diagnosis isn't like that. It's life changing and monumental. There's no harm in asking your autistic friend or loved one how they feel about their autism diagnosis periodically – whether it's changed what they do, where they work, how they manage their self-care, how it affected them as a child, and how it tallies with past experiences that the person found challenging, because of their autism and the way it coloured their experiences. There's every chance that the conversation will be appreciated! (Maybe make it on email, schedule any phone calls in a diary, in triplicate, or ensure it takes place in a real-world, quiet, subtly-lit place with just you two present... we autists like to be picky about the logistics of conversation!)

The autist's view

This chapter has of course been written from my view (and as such isn't necessarily relevant for other autists too), so this section will be succinct. But I feel it is worth emphasising that an autism diagnosis is unlike most other diagnoses, and warrants a different approach from friends and families. There's a danger that (1) as a newly diagnosed autist, it becomes your new special interest, and you start to bore people with your new-found knowledge and viewpoint. This is a good reason why people may not want to enquire about how it affects you. And (2) that people are confused or disbelieving of the diagnosis, holding the dated view that all autists are like Raymond from the film Rainman. This can lead to a dismissive view that somehow your diagnosing clinician was wrong, you are 'only mildly autistic so it presumably doesn't affect you much' (see the chapter: 'L is for labels and language'), or that autism is simply a differentiating factor like being green-eyed, shorter than your peers or left-handed, that doesn't directly affect you on a day to day basis. (Like being 'ditsy' or 'quirky').

Hopefully if you have read the preceding chapters, you will appreciate that autism is not a differentiating factor, but a lifelong way of experiencing the world that can bring many challenges and difficulties, including marginalisation. It can bring unique experiences and benefits, however.

Z is for zzz

The zzz here refers to sleep, and covers both sleeping and dreaming. The National Autistic Society (NAS) maintains that many people on the autistic spectrum are likely to suffer from disturbed sleep patterns at some point in their lives, recognising that there is very little research evidence on the effectiveness of most treatments for sleep problems in autistic people. '*Reasons for this [disturbed sleep patterns] could include difficulty settling, winding down and going to sleep; waking repeatedly during the night, or having difficulty getting back to sleep after waking up; increased anxiety or an inability to relax, causing insomnia; irregular secretion of the sleep hormone melatonin, which regulates sleep patterns, or having atypical circadian (body clock) rhythms; sensory differences, such as increased sensitivity to blue light, or sensitivity to certain sounds or white noise, which may be upsetting or distracting; hypersomnia, e.g. sleeping too much, linked to increased exhaustion potentially caused by the additional stress that autistic people experience in social situations,*' the NAS states on its website. (Further below in this chapter, this author considers the fact that autistic children are said to have high levels of neurons in their amygdala, which has the potential to affect their dream-states and their quality of sleep.)

Research Autism's '*Essential Guide to Sleep Problems and Autism*' (see: *www.tiny.cc/AutismSleep*) notes that most of the treatments used to help autistic people with sleep problems are the same as those designed to help anyone with sleep problems, and include (but aren't limited to): Bedtime fading, e.g. going to bed at progressively earlier times; scheduled awakening, e.g. waking someone up at predetermined times; sleep restriction, e.g. limiting the time someone spends in bed; extinction procedures, e.g. removing parental involvement during bedtime disruptions. The organisation, whose information service is now part of the NAS, adds that biomedical approaches include the use of medications (such as melatonin), dietary supplements (such as valerian), and diets that exclude foodstuffs (such as additives).

Other treatments include aromatherapy, exercise programmes, homeopathy, light therapy, massage, weighted blankets and yoga. (As stated in this book's preface, individuals should always seek the care of a qualified doctor or relevant healthcare professional to discuss their own personal healthcare status, or that of their families.)

The resource Ambitious About Autism lists a few fantastic theories in an article entitled 'Sleep' (see: *www.tiny.cc/SLEEP*), which include the theory that autistic children perhaps don't release melatonin at the right times of day; that sensory sensitivities make it harder to relax; that social communication difficulties make it hard for a child to explain why something's bothering them and preventing them from sleeping; that the well-known difficulties in autists with transitioning from one state or activity to another can cause problems with sleeping; that autists' rigid thoughts and behaviour patterns may require a particular ritual or object every time they get into bed; and that some autistic children with autism have co-existing medical conditions that can affect sleep.

Moving on from sleeping, within this chapter, this author would like to include the following section on dreaming, sourced from *www.spectra.blog*, and written as a first-person perspective:

I had a strange dream last night. The actor Al Pacino was at an event I was attending, and was acting as a financial advisor for a friend. It was a fun dream. I don't remember the 'ins and outs' of the dream now. But: I awoke with a question blazing: do autists 'dream autistic'? Are we aware of our 'autisticness' in our dreams? Autistic people are thought to dream differently from neurotypical (NT) or non- autistic individuals. (E.g. supposedly with fewer characters and social interactions in their dreams – see more details further within this chapter). But, do they dream as autistic people? Or do they dream as NTs; e.g. projecting their belief of what life would be/feel like, as an NT person?

Autists are obviously on a spectrum across the autistic population, e.g. with no two autistic people presenting with exactly the same traits, behaviours and challenges – however, this author also thinks that autists are on a further, individual spectrum. E.g. in simplified language, we can feel more or less atypical on different days, depending on the challenges facing us, and our ability to function, in the face of these challenges. (This is what the 'Spectra.blog' scales logo on the cover of the book represents). So, on some days as an autist, one can feel relatively functional. E.g. we may be able to hold (our own version of) eye contact, get through the day in our jobs, hold conversations that would be deemed 'typical', and feel quite good about ourselves. On other days, our senses are overloaded, we're 'peopled out', and our executive functioning and working memory is questionable at best. So, if we're like this in everyday life, e.g. the autistic elements of our brain taking the forefront on some days, and the more NT aspects driving our neurological train on other days, it stands to reason that our sleeping brain is adaptable.

American doctor and research author Francesca Siclari has questioned whether the dreaming and waking elements of our brains are much more similar than we previously imagined. *"[Perhaps] because they partially recruit the same areas, for the same type of experiences,"* she said. Her co-authored study, published in the journal Nature Neuroscience (source: *www.tiny.cc/Siclari*), found that dreaming about faces was linked to increased high-frequency activity in the region of the brain involved in face recognition, with dreams involving spatial perception, movement and thinking similarly linked to regions of the brain that handle such tasks when awake.

The whole brain is actually active during dreams, from the brain stem to the cortex. The sleep-wake cycle and is controlled by the reticular activating system, whose circuits run from the brain stem, through the thalamus to the cortex. The limbic system in the mid-brain deals with emotions in both waking and dreaming, and includes the amygdala, which is especially active during dreams, and governs social and emotional behaviour. The cortex is said to be responsible for the content of dreams, and the visual cortex is especially active at this time. A study published in 'Experimental Neurobiology' found that the brain areas associated with social communication and interaction challenges are referred to as the 'social brain area', and include the superior temporal sulcus (STS) and its adjoining areas, which include the amygdala. (Source: *www.tiny.cc/yonsei*). In autistic people (in general, not specifically linked to dream-states), there's said to be increased patterns of brain activity in the amygdala region, an area thought to be linked to autist's social deficits. One study – (*www.tiny.cc/AmygdalaASD*), now admittedly a little dated, found that brain activation in autistic adults remained elevated long after similar brain regions of 'typically developed' adults had stopped being activated, when exposed to a series of pictures of human faces. The study discovered hyperexcitability or over-arousal of the amygdala in autistic individuals, suggesting that neurons in the amygdala are firing more than expected in autists.

Another, more recent study (into anxiety) proposed that: "*It should not be surprising [that] there is substantial evidence that the structure and function of the amygdala in autism is altered.*" (Source: *www.tiny.cc/AHalladay*). A further study found that autistic children have too many neurons early on, and then appear to lose those neurons as they become adults, describing an '*abnormal trajectory of development*' in the autistic amygdala that could link to the high levels of anxiety seen in autists. (Source: *www.tiny.cc/A_Avino*). Incidentally, this latter study does not have converse findings to the earlier one listed (*www.tiny.cc/AmygdalaASD*) – it finds that there are simply less neurons in adult autists; while the first study mentioned found that the existing neurons in the amygdala, no matter how many or few there were, *fired more* in autists.

But back to dreaming. We know that the amygdala, which is especially active during dreams, and governs social and emotional behaviour, could have a different developmental trajectory in autists. It seems that autistic children have high levels of neurons in their amygdala, which surely affects their dream-states and their quality of sleep? Personally, I don't think that I 'dream autistic'. If I try to analyse it, I believe that in my dreams, I am presenting as an NT person. Is this: (a) because I am late-diagnosed, and my subconscious hasn't yet got the memo? Or is it (b) because the part of my brain that creates my dreams is somehow 'less autistic' than other areas, for want of a more scientific and less un-PC description? This theory doesn't seem to stand up to scrutiny – one study found a 'significant reduction' of fractional anisotropy, which can be simplified as a measure of density and diameter, in several areas of autistic brains studied, including areas of the cortex. (Source: *www.tiny.cc/Connectopathy*). And as we have seen, the amygdala is widely thought to be affected in autists. Science seemingly doesn't back up my theory that I don't 'dream autistic'. It seems that the 'dreaming brain' and the 'waking brain' are similar, because they recruit the same areas of the brain for the same type of experiences. So, if we lack social skills in real life, we will probably lack them when dreaming, it is proposed. (Obviously, it is also difficult to analyse one's dreams subjectively, when one is awake!)

Older theories propose that our dreams predominantly occur during REM (rapid eye movement) sleep, controlled by the 'reticular activating system', whose circuits run from the brain stem through the thalamus to the cortex. However, the research already mentioned, and published in the journal Nature Neuroscience (source: *www.tiny.cc/Siclari*), found that dreams also occur during non-REM sleep. Analysis of this study's volunteers' EEG recordings revealed that dreaming was linked to a drop in low-frequency activity in a region at the back of the brain, dubbed by the researchers the 'posterior cortical hot zone' – a region that includes visual areas, as well as those involved in integrating the senses.

There have been specific studies relating to autistic people and dreaming – an older study, published in the Journal of Autism & Developmental Disorders, found that autistic participants had fewer recollections of dreaming, fewer bad dreams and fewer emotions. Dream content narratives were shorter in autistic participants than in controls, while autistic participants also reported fewer settings, objects, characters, social interactions, activities, and emotions. (Source: *www.tiny.cc/Daoust*). So, we know that autistic people are thought to dream differently (e.g. supposedly fewer characters and social interactions in their dreams). But it is interesting to ponder – do they dream as autistic people – are they aware of their real-life 'autisticness', in their dreams – e.g. self-aware? Or do they dream as NTs? There's no way of ascertaining answers here. One respondent to the original online article that this section of the chapter is sourced from, Luna, told this author: "*I'm autistic. In my dreams, I am usually still myself, so that means I'm autistic too. I stim in my dreams. In my best dreams, I can fly, and I am free to be me. I actually have less emotional regulation skills in my dreams, so I might be perceived as 'more autistic' because I meltdown in ways that I don't in real life. Of course, autism isn't linear, so there's no such thing as 'more autistic'; just 'less immune to stress', I suppose. Or perhaps it's just the fact that my nightmares can be intense. I am not like the people in the study. While my dreams are less social, they are highly intricate and lengthy, full of detailed places. I have a very rich dreaming life.*"

The autist's view

As an adult, I don't suffer too badly with sleeping, although due to my sensory sensitivities, I require a completely dark, quiet room to get to sleep, and I am easily woken by light. Earplugs and eye-masks are wonderful things! However (reflecting the theories about excessive brain neurons described above), I suffered terribly with disrupted sleep as a child, regularly experiencing nightmares and the odd bouts of sleep talking and sleep walking. I think Ambitious About Autism has hit the nail on the head with their suggestions for the potential causes for sleep problems in autists. For me as a child, my issues with transitioning from one state or activity to another, and my rigid thought patterns that led me to need a verbal ritual that I would say to myself each night, seemingly contributed to my sleep difficulties.

Rigid thought patterns, and that autistic trait of 'not letting things go', or hyper-focussing on an issue (see the chapter: '*O is for obsession*'), certainly fuelled my nightmares as a child, and well into adulthood. However, talking therapy and hypno-therapy in my 30s quickly identified some emotional issues I was holding onto, and allowed the nightmares to (for the most part), cease.

Anxiety is surely a big factor for autists too. As I wrote in the chapter: '*A is for anxiety*', if you are autistic, anxiety can really be considered to be part of your autistic DNA. On a blog for the mental health charity MIND (see: *www.mind.org.uk*), one author writes: 'When you're suffering from anxiety, your adrenaline levels are constantly running higher than normal. It's essentially like being put through the 'fight or flight' response 24/7, for no discernible reason.' Of course, this state isn't conducive to sleep.

Interestingly, I occasionally experienced an unwelcome, trance-like state as I was approaching sleep as a child, that I now believe was linked to being autistic. It wasn't a nightmare as such (as I wasn't asleep), but was nightmarish. I can only describe it as a vivid sensory experience, when (with my eyes open), my visual, auditory and kinaesthetic senses were skewed, like a painting being stretched. Everything was amplified, and I remember being horribly 'stuck' in the experience.

On the subject of dreams, mine have always predominantly been lucid (e.g. so I am aware I am dreaming). They're still frequently vivid. Like Luna, I don't really fit the results found in the study on dreaming (see: *www.tiny.cc/Daoust*) that found that autistic participants had fewer recollections of dreaming and fewer bad dreams. On the subject of how emotional my dreams are, that's also hard to quantify!

This final chapter closes the A-Z content of the book, so the author hopes readers have gained some insight from the title's contents.

A thousand souls
a poem about autism

In a lifetime we're privileged to meet eighty thousand souls.
Around a thousand have autism; still with dreams and goals.

On the autistic spectrum, processing is a chore.
Not necessarily 'impaired'; nor diseased to their core.

Educators, practitioners, families and friends
Lacking understanding, yet on them the autist depends.

How many of this thousand that we'll meet, have diagnosis?
Many are still unaware; yet we share symbiosis.

Without autism, computers, smart phones, tech are less
enduring.
Pioneers forging 'aspie' paths: Tesler, Gates and Turing.

So, what's the difference in these souls, the thousand that
we'll meet?
Maybe sensory challenges, to light and sound and heat.

A difficulty blending in; socialisation quirks.
Different communication styles; a trait that sometimes irks.

But at their core, a simple truth – differences in processing.
A brain speed sometimes fast or slow – constantly assessing.

These souls, often creative: scientists, artists, writers.
Musicians, sculptors, poets, whose creations still delight us.

Many leading figures; Michelangelo, Warhol, Mozart
Are thought to have been autistic – perhaps it drove their art.

Yet those with autism don't want reverence; handling with kid glove.
Just inclusion, acceptance, and a healthy dose of love.

Much less ignorance: 'Well. We're all autistic aren't we?'
No. And while we're at it, that young autist isn't naughty.

Another irk. 'You must be high functioning', peers say.
It's called 'autistic masking', to get one through the day.

So, these one thousand souls, that we'll meet throughout our life.
They're our bosses, neighbours, workmates; a husband and a wife.

The literal thinkers, loyal peers, problem solvers great.
The listeners, grounded cynics, the friends we truly rate.

Their daily struggles are unseen. Until the curtains close.
Their difference in processing results in crashing lows.

So education, acceptance and awareness are our goals
To understand autism, and embrace these thousand souls.

—Kathy Carter

Printed in Great Britain
by Amazon

41069494R00132